T0318502

Cambridge Elements ≡

Elements in Pragmatics
edited by
Jonathan Culpeper
Lancaster University, UK
Michael Haugh
University of Queensland, Australia

PRAGMATICS, (IM) POLITENESS, AND INTERGROUP COMMUNICATION

A Multilayered, Discursive Analysis of Cancel Culture

Pilar Garcés-Conejos Blitvich
The University of North Carolina at Charlotte

CAMBRIDGE
UNIVERSITY PRESS

Shaftesbury Road, Cambridge CB2 8EA, United Kingdom

One Liberty Plaza, 20th Floor, New York, NY 10006, USA

477 Williamstown Road, Port Melbourne, VIC 3207, Australia

314–321, 3rd Floor, Plot 3, Splendor Forum, Jasola District Centre,
New Delhi – 110025, India

103 Penang Road, #05–06/07, Visioncrest Commercial, Singapore 238467

Cambridge University Press is part of Cambridge University Press & Assessment,
a department of the University of Cambridge.

We share the University's mission to contribute to society through the pursuit of
education, learning and research at the highest international levels of excellence.

www.cambridge.org
Information on this title: www.cambridge.org/9781009494830

DOI: 10.1017/9781009184373

First published 2024

A catalogue record for this publication is available from the British Library.

ISBN 978-1-009-49483-0 Hardback
ISBN 978-1-009-18438-0 Paperback
ISSN 2633-6464 (online)
ISSN 2633-6456 (print)

Cambridge University Press & Assessment has no responsibility for the persistence
or accuracy of URLs for external or third-party internet websites referred to in this
publication and does not guarantee that any content on such websites is, or will
remain, accurate or appropriate.

Pragmatics, (Im)politeness, and Intergroup Communication

A Multilayered, Discursive Analysis of *Cancel Culture*

Elements in Pragmatics

DOI: 10.1017/9781009184373
First published online: January 2024

Pilar Garcés-Conejos Blitvich
The University of North Carolina at Charlotte

Author for correspondence: Pilar Garcés-Conejos Blitvich, pgblitvi@
charlotte.edu

Abstract: This Element argues and presents the bases for pragmatics/
(im)politeness to become intergroup-oriented so as to be able to
consider interactions in which social identities are salient or are
essentially collective in nature, such as Cancel Culture (CC). CC is a form
of ostracism involving the collective withdrawal of support and
concomitant group exclusion of individuals perceived as having
behaved in ways construed as immoral and thus displaying disdain for
group normativity. To analyze this type of collective phenomenon,
a three-layered model that tackles CC manifestations at the macro,
meso, and micro levels is used. Results problematize extant
conceptualizations of CC-mostly focused on the macro level-and
describe it as a Big C Conversation, whose meso-level practices need to
be understood as genre-ecology, and where identity reduction,
im/politeness, and moral emotions synergies are key to understand
group entitativity and agency.

Keywords: Im/politeness, Cancel Culture, Intergroup communication, Moral
emotions, genres

ISBNs: 9781009494830 (HB), 9781009184380 (PB), 9781009184373 (OC)
ISSNs: 2633-6464 (online), 2633-6456 (print)

Contents

1 Introduction

This Element's main argument is that pragmatics, more specifically (im)politeness research, needs to be more cognizant of intergroup communication, understood as those cases in which social – rather than individual – identity is salient (Giles, 2012). The thrust behind it is that there seem to be many communicative phenomena that simply cannot be accounted for in interpersonal terms but are collective in nature and should be understood by recourse to a group. This is true of interactions when those involved occupy positions afforded to them by a recognized social identity – such as employer/employee in a corporate meeting or Black Lives Matter supporter in a demonstration. Further, there are certain actions that cannot be performed at the individual level because they emanate from the group and, as such, need to be carried out by it (or emissaries acting on its behalf). Among these, we find groups' reprisal to members' breaching of social norms. Social norms are, in themselves, a quintessential group phenomenon. By displaying overt (or at least perceived) disdain for group norms, a member may be (intentionally or perceived as) signaling that they do not conform to the group's cultural practices and thus be seen as potentially harmful to group life. Often, different types of retribution for infringement ensue which, on occasion, may be quite severe, resulting in group exclusion and ostracism (Tomasello et al., 2012).

Group exclusion practices are at the heart of what has become known as *cancel culture (CC)*, here understood as a blanket term used to refer to a modern form of ostracism in which someone (the *cancelee*) is thrust out of social or professional circles as a result of being fired, deplatformed or boycotted by others, the *cancelers*. The *cancelee* is also subjected to public shaming and censorship and often faces serious financial, and even legal, repercussions for having engaged in different types of behavior perceived as immoral. Morality is closely connected to social norms and, thus, to group goals and collective intentionality (Tomasello, 2018). While the fact that *CC* exists is not controversial, what varies substantially is whether it is seen either as (i) a way to keep individuals accountable and provide a voice to traditionally disenfranchised groups (first wave) or (ii) an unjust form of punishment and censorship that aims at undermining, among others, freedom of speech (second wave; Romano, 2021; Section 4.2). Here, without taking a stance on whether its goals are laudable or censurable, *cancelation* is viewed as an intrinsically aggressive off/online set of group practices whose main goals are public exposure, group exclusion, punishment of target *cancelees,* and social regulation. *CC*-associated practices can thus be categorized as a type of *reactive aggression* (Allen & Anderson, 2017) since they involve retaliation to perceived offense with further offense (Garcés-Conejos Blitvich, 2022b). Therefore, this Element is firmly anchored in the subfield of pragmatics that analyzes understandings of (im)politeness and language aggression and conflict (Culpeper, 2011).

By focusing on their interconnections, this Element aims at advancing our knowledge of intergroup communication, on the one hand, and of *CC*, on the other. With very few exceptions (Bouvier, 2020; Garcés-Conejos Blitvich, 2021, 2022a, 2022b; Haugh, 2022), *CC* analyses have taken a macro-level approach and, as a result, may have painted this social phenomenon with a thick brush, many of its idiosyncrasies glossed over (Garcés-Conejos Blitvich, 2021). Indeed, some are calling for "qualitative accounts of the specific practices and interactional dynamics at play" and a more ethnographic approach to these phenomena (Ng, 2020: 623).

By taking a discursive pragmatics approach to the data (Garcés-Conejos Blitvich 2010c, 2013; Garcés-Conejos Blitvich & Sifianou, 2019) that involves macro/meso/micro-level analyses, this Element scrutinizes the complexities of three case studies of *cancelation* involving three American women from different walks of life: Congresswoman Liz Cheney, comedian Ellen Degeneres, and sports commentator Rachel Nichols.[1] Thus, the study has a USA focus. Importantly, although CC is claimed to be experienced elsewhere (Velasco, 2020), its origins are quintessentially American (see Section 4). To carry out the study, Fairclough's (2003) discourse in social practice model is taken as a starting point, since it nicely incorporates these three levels of sociological inquiry: discourses (macro-level units) are instantiated in genres (meso-level units), which are, in turn realized at the micro-level (via different types of linguistic – and other semiotic – [inter]actions) many of which are entextualized, such as the user-generated comments in the corpus. More specifically, *CC*, at the macro-level, is understood as a Big C Conversation (Gee, 2014) and will be distinguished from the processes involved in the now *recognizable* (Blommaert et al., 2018; Garfinkel, 2002) practice of *cancelation* (Saint-Louis, 2021) whereby individuals get canceled, which is properly realized at the meso-level via a complex genre ecology (Spinuzzi & Zachy, 2000) and at the micro-level by genre-specific constrained interactions. Although research (Saint-Louis, 2021) insightfully pointed to the conceptual differences between *CC* and *cancelation*, no discourse-based analysis to date has offered a detailed description of the meso-level practices deployed to carry out *cancelation*. From this perspective, this Element contributes to advancing discursive pragmatics/(im)politeness, as these fields have traditionally paid more attention to the macro and micro-levels.

---

[1] Three middle aged/white women were chosen as targets to homogenize the sample. However, this Element looks at *CC* from an ideological rather than gendered perspective.

Regarding the micro-level, interactions that realize the genre commonly known as online comments, a sizeable analytic corpus extracted from the *CC* Corpus, were qualitatively scrutinized to gain insights into intergroup communication. Although, as mentioned, *CC* is not just an online phenomenon, its online manifestations do carry significant weight as initiators and continuators of *cancelation*. In addition, they provide prime sites for the analysis of group behavior and intergroup communication. In part, this has to do with the anonymity afforded by online platforms: anonymity enhances social identity (Reicher et al., 1995). Further, digital communication allows for the creation of a multiplicity of diverse groups (from very *thick* to very *light*, Blommaert, 2017a) and affords the necessary "scenes," online free spaces (Fine, 2012; Rao & Dutta, 2012), for these groups to assemble and carry out different actions related to the group's goals. These goals are closely tied to their claimed social identity (Fine, 2012) and collective intentionality (Jankovic & Ludwig, 2017). In this respect, *CC* is related to what has been described as *light* groups, a staple of online communication. The present study also contributes to understanding of how such groups become agents (Tuomela, 2013).

Concerning *CC*, this Element helps to dispel some commonly held beliefs: such as that *CC* is entirely an online phenomenon or that it is univocal in its direction: led by *woke* mobs that seek the same goal. Indeed, conservatives also engage in a type of straightforward *cancelation* typically associated with the first wave of *CC* (as Cheney's case illustrates). Results confirm that *CC* has evolved since its inception and support claims of a second wave (Romano, 2021) in which the *ultimate canceller* – that is, corporations, political parties, and so on – rather than the *cancelees* themselves, becomes the target. However, this second wave is not necessarily conservative-led. A third type of *cancelation* (not associated with a specific political persuasion) targets both the *cancelee and* the *ultimate canceler*. Further, from the analysis of complex genre ecologies deployed to carry out *cancelation*s, *CC* emerges as prime example of the off/online nexus of post-digital societies (Blommaert, 2019) and will be here seen from the perspective of augmented reality which understands the digital and the physical as highly enmeshed (Jurgenson, 2011).

Additionally, although group phenomena such as social exclusion/ostracism have received considerable attention (Foucault, 1996; Hoover & Milner, 1998; Peters & Beasley, 2014) for the most part, little is known about how these exclusionary practices are carried out at the micro-level. Significantly, these rituals are approached here spatially, from a geo-semiotics perspective. Following Goffman (1963b), Scollon and Wong Scollon (2003) and Blommaert (2013), off/online space is understood as being regulative and, thus, historical and political. Further, applying the tenets of emotional geographies (Davidson et al., 2005), the online free spaces here under scrutiny are seen as transforming into "other-condemning/suffering" (Haidt, 2003) emotional spaces where behavior considered antinormative (i.e., triggers that set *cancelation* in motion) is, in turn, un/civilly evaluated. Furthermore, said spaces become moralizing sites about offline normativity where the dark side of morality emerges full force (Monroe & Ashby Plant, 2019; Rempala et al., 2020). Relatedly, results reveal a close connection between morality, shared emotions, and aggressive retaliation via (im)politeness.

This Element is organized as follows: Section 2 discusses the hurdles to and proposes a model for a pragmatics/(im)politeness of intergroup communication. Section 3 pays close attention to the meso-level, the level of groups, and discusses how online spaces facilitate the formation of light groupings. Section 4 begins the empirical part of the Element by tackling the macro-level exploration of *CC* and includes an overview of the three case studies that are probed in the meso/micro-levels of analysis, the foci of Sections 5 and 6, respectively. For ease of reading, a methods section related to each discursive level starts the dedicated sections. In Section 7, analysis driven responses are provided to the guiding research questions (Section 3.1) and future venues for further research are discussed.

2 A Pragmatics of Intergroup Communication

Pragmatics, both utterance and discourse based, has mostly focused on interpersonal communication (Haugh et al., 2013; Locher & Graham, 2010), in which the personal/individual identity of the interlocutors is most salient. Personal identity refers to self-categories which define the individual as a unique person, regarding their individual differences from other (ingroup) members. For its part, intergroup communication was defined as "interactions where participants' group identities – their clans, cliques, unions, generations, families, and so on – almost entirely dictate the conversational dynamics; speakers' idiosyncratic characteristics here would be almost immaterial" (Giles, 2012: 3). The boundaries between personal and social identity are porous: group/social identity is the portion of an individual's self-concept derived from perceived membership in a relevant social group (Tajfel & Turner, 1979/2006). Despite pragmatics scholarship leaning toward the former, the latter plays a major (some argue even more highly pervasive) role in communication. As Giles (2012: 3) noted, "Henri Tajfel had always argued ... that at least 70% of so-called interpersonal interactions were actually highly intergroup in nature ... this could perhaps even turn to be an underestimate."

Saying that pragmatics has mostly focused on interpersonal communication does not mean that there are no studies in which intergroup communication figures prominently. For example, within (im)politeness research, there has been substantial work done on communication in professional genres: service encounters (Márquez Reiter & Bou-Franch, 2017), health encounters (Locher & Schnurr, 2017); courtroom discourse (Lakoff, 1988), political discourse (Harris, 2001) and on gender (Holmes, 2013; Lakoff, 1975; Mills, 2003), all instances of social identity being salient. The same could be said about intercultural/cross-cultural/contrastive pragmatics that focus on national, ethnic, or language/culture groups (Blum-Kulka, House & Kasper, 1989; Márquez-Reiter & Placencia, 2005; Sifianou, 1999). To a lesser degree, links have been established between other social identities and (im)politeness. For instance, religion (Ariff, 2012), age (Bella, 2009), social class (Salmani-Nodoushan, 2007), and race (Morgan, 2010).

However, intergroup communication has often been approached from an interpersonal perspective and the constraints placed on communication by occurring intergroup have, in my view, not been sufficiently explored. This may be due, as Blommaert (2017a) discusses in his review of Durkheim's ideas, to the dominance of Rational Choice Theory, a spin-off of Methodological Individualism. Methodological Individualism argues that every human activity can be reduced to individual levels of subjectivity in action (such as interests, intentions, motives, concerns, decisions) even if it is eminently social. Rational Choice is driven by the maximization of individual profit (material and symbolic) and proceeds by means of calculated intentional and rational decisions by individuals.

It is not difficult to trace strong parallels between the tenets of Methodological Individualism and those of foundational models and theories of pragmatics, such as Brown and Levinson's (1987) politeness, and their rational Model Person, Leech's (1983) characterization of pragmatics as eminently strategic and thus rhetorical, a means to an end, and the speaker-centeredness that dominates Speech Act Theory. Further, Blommaert (2017a: 17) points out that, in its most radical versions of Rational Choice, "people never seem to communicate or to communicate only in dyadic logical dialogue." Dyadic communication has also been a staple in pragmatics, perhaps another hurdle to tackling genres that involve collective engagement and polylogal interaction (Bou-Franch & Garcés-Conejos Blitvich, 2014). All in all, with such a strong bias toward individualism, it has not been easy to conceptualize the "social fact," that is, the collective in Durkheim's terms, in pragmatic terms.

In the next three sections, I propose a framework to overcome potential hurdles to a group pragmatics/(im)politeness. Although it mostly focuses on (im)politeness, due to this Element's relational emphasis, it can be extended to other pragmatic phenomena (such as explicated/implicated meaning which is heavily influenced by the meso-level and individual/social identity claims/attribution). At the core of my proposal lies the recommendation to make pragmatics discursive in its orientation (see Garcés-Conejos Blitvich 2010c, 2013; Garcés-Conejos Blitvich & Sifianou, 2019) and the related need to explore the meso-level of sociological enquiry (much less researched than the macro and micro-levels in pragmatics scholarship). The meso-level happens to be the level of practices, and thus of groups, and, therefore, essential to understand collective action and intentionality (key components of the proposed framework). In this respect, Culpeper and Haugh (2021: 323) argue that "meso-level concepts do have an important role to play in teasing out the role context plays in assessments of (im) politeness. Indeed, we suspect that it is at the meso-level that the most important work in theorizing (im)politeness is most likely to continue." In addition, especially for research on (im)politeness, a discursive pragmatics opens the door to deeper considerations of identity in relation to face, central constructs of (im) politeness models, as identity is at the core of discourses.

2.1 Overcoming Potential Hurdles to a Pragmatics(im)politeness of Groups

2.1.1 Face and Identity

The lack of exploration of intergroup communication within pragmatics/(im) politeness may be due to several factors. One of them being that, in general, most research has not necessarily focused on identity but on *face*. Face, the inspiration behind the core concept in Brown and Levinson's (1987) framework, was defined by Goffman as "the positive social value a person effectively claims for himself by the line others assume he has taken during a particular contact. Face is an image of self delineated in terms of approved social attributes" (1955/ 1967: 5). As Garcés-Conejos Blitvich (2013) argued, Goffman conceptualized face as being tied to a line (a role, an identity).[2] However, Brown and Levinson's construal of face altered its essence, as they separated face from *line* and presented it as a primarily cognitive construct possessed by a rational *Model Person*. This focus on individualism is one of the reasons why their politeness theory drew some of the earliest critiques from scholars from collectivism-oriented cultures (Matsumoto, 1988; Nwoye, 1992) and the argument behind taking into consideration discernment along with strategic politeness (Ide, 1989). It has also been a deterrent for advancing the study of intergroup communication.

Relatedly, another reason leading to a dearth of research on intergroup communication can be related to how face is further conceptualized, more specifically as to whether it is taken to be accrued over time, which means it can be attached to groups (Sifianou 2011; Wang & Spencer-Oatey, 2015) or is emergent in interaction (Arundale, 1999; Haugh, 2007), in which case it cannot be shared by a group (since it is unlikely that all members would be interacting concurrently).

---

[2] Goffman dropped the term 'face' and substituted it with identity in the bulk of his work.

Although this is a key conceptual point that needs to be tackled to theorize intergroup communication (see Haugh et al., 2013 discussion of relational histories), it has not received significant attention within (im)politeness research. Some exceptions are Hatfield and Hahn (2014) and, more recently, O'Driscoll (2017: 104) who concluded that "it is again not clear how group face … is to be distinguished from (the self-evidently valid concept of) a group's reputation / image / identity." However, he went on to cite Spencer-Oatey's (2005) "social identity face," the desire for acknowledgment of one's social identities or roles (e.g., group leader, valued customer), as appearing to have distinct meaning.

In my view, the problems that face, as understood in the literature discussed, poses in relation to groups can be bypassed by resorting, instead, to a closely related concept: identity or the social positioning of self and other (Bucholtz & Hall, 2005: 586). Although face and identity are both significantly related to the construction and presentation of self (Goffman, 1955/1967), they have – for the most part – been the cornerstones of different research traditions. One fundamental difference between (im)politeness and identity scholarship is that the latter has devoted considerable thought to whether identity is accrued or emergent in interaction. There seems to be quite universal consensus in post-structural/discursive approaches to identity in this respect: identity is discursive, intersubjectively co-constructed, *emergent* in interaction (for instance, it involves those very ephemeral subject positions that we occupy in unfolding discourse and that make up stance), but also *durable* (Bucholtz & Hall, 2005).

Identities are durable, not because individuals have essential or primal identities, but because dialogically constructed identities are recreated in multiple local practices where they make sense and create meaning (Holland & Lave, 2001). Butler (1990) refers to a process of *sedimentation* whereby people repeatedly draw on resources that gradually build up an appearance of fixed identities. Whereas it is true that certain aspects of person, role and social identities are more stable, even those are always overlapping with each other and constantly changing (Burke & Stets, 2009). Barker and Galasinski (2001: 31) sum up this well when they state: "Identities are both unstable *and* temporarily stabilized by social practice and regular, predictable behaviour." From this unstable/stabilized, emergent/durable perspective, it is conceptually quite unproblematic to tie identity (and face, as we will see later in this section) to groups.

In the mid-to-late 2000s, identity started to be presented alongside face in the definitions of (im)politeness. Scholars also began enquiring about its relationship with face and introducing (im)politeness studies to the frameworks developed for the analysis of identity, arguing for their relevance to (im)politeness research (see among others Spencer-Oatey, 2007; Locher, 2008; Garcés-Conejos Blitvich, 2009, 2013; Garcés-Conejos Blitvich & Sifianou, 2017;

Garcés-Conejos Blitvich & Georgakopoulou, 2021). Those scholars who argued for a more multi-disciplinary approach to the study of (im)politeness phenomena saw identity models as a means to achieve that goal, due to the close relationship between face, identity, and self-presentation. Proposed ways of advancing the field can be summarized as follows:

a. (Im)politeness manifestations/assessments can be tied to identity (co)construction, not just to face.
b. Identity and face are inseparable, as they co-constitute each other.
c. (Im)politeness can be analyzed as an index in identity construction.
d. Models developed for the analysis of identity construction can be fruitfully applied to the study of (im)politeness (Garcés-Conejos Blitvich & Sifianou, 2017: 238).

Since then, identity has either replaced face as a core concept in (im)politeness research or has been seen as essential to grasp what face entails, as face needs vary depending on the identity being co-constructed by an agent engaged in a specific practice: that is, an agent's face needs as a *mother* differ substantially from those of the same agent's face as a *surgeon*, or as a *bridge player*. In this practice-based approach, face and identity are viewed as difficult to tease apart in interaction and as co-constituting each other (Joseph, 2013; Miller, 2013). Crucially, agents engaged in practice may claim or be attributed either an individual or a social identity and its concomitant face needs and thus group (social) identity is seen, from this perspective, as unproblematically tied to face. Indeed, the concept of self-esteem so closely connected to face is foremost in the conceptualization of social identity as discussed by Tajfel (1979) who proposed that the groups (e.g., social class, family, and football team) which people belonged to are an important source of pride and self-worth. Relatedly, Goffman (1959: 85) reconceptualized his framework in making the team, rather than the individual, the basic unit of the interactional order. The goal of the team is to help teammates maintain the line they have selected. In this sense, teams/groups provide us with a sense of belonging to the social world.

2.1.2 Collective Intentionality and Action

Yet, another motive behind the inattention toward intergroup communication in pragmatics/(im)politeness may have to do with the major role that intentionality has played in pragmatic understandings of the conveyance and interpretation of meaning (especially in the Cognitive-Philosophical foundational models and theories of the field, which primed speaker-meaning, such as Speech Act Theory, Grice's Cooperative Principle, etc.).

Although its role as an a priori concept has been questioned (Haugh, 2008a), most pragmatic scholars still see intention as playing a (varying) influential role in communication (Culpeper, 2011; different contributions to *Journal of Pragmatics 179*, 2021). As Haugh (2008b) discussed, traditional views relate intentionality to *individual* utterances/speakers, but a higher-order intention would need to be attached to larger stretches of discourse. In addition, if intentionality is understood as co-constructed among participants in interaction, it may be appropriate to consider a *we-intention* as also being applicable (Haugh, 2008a; Haugh & Jaszczolt, 2012). However, Haugh (2008b) saw *we-intention*, as described in the then extant literature, as static and not adequately capturing the emergent nature of inferential work underpinning cooperative activities, such as conversation.

An important, for this Element, related question is whether we should appeal to an ontology of group agents, i.e., when a team plays, is the team just made up of individuals coordinating in search of a common goal or is the team itself that plays? This question has been tackled mostly from the point of view of philosophy and resulted into two opposing camps: individualism and collectivism. Individualism understands and explains both individual action and social ontology resorting to individuals and their relations and interactions. For its part, collectivism argues that there are genuinely emergent social phenomena, such as social objects (i.e., groups), states, facts, events, and processes (Tuomela, 2013).

When dealing with shared intentions, more specifically, two opposing views are upheld: (i) those who spouse reductive views of shared intention, that is, attributing an intention to *us* – as in a group – can be undertaken by resorting to concepts related to individual action/intention, and (ii) those who disagree with this position and hold non-reductive views and understand *we-intentions* as involving an irreducible *we-mode*. The *we-mode* approach (Tuomela, 2007, 2011) is predicated on the crucial distinction between acting as a group member guided by the group ethos versus acting as a private person.

In more recent work, Tuomela (2017: 16) reviewed some of the central accounts of non-reductive views, namely those espoused by Gilbert (1989), Searle (2010) and himself (Tuomela, 2013), and described them along the following lines:

> Groups (including collectively constructed group agents) as social systems (interconnected structures formed out of individuals and their interrelations) seem in many cases to be ontologically emergent (viz. involve qualitatively new features as compared with the individualistic basis) and in this sense irreducible to the individualistic properties of our commonsense framework of agency and persons … on conceptual grounds collective states are not reducible to individualist states.

Despite some commonalities, Tuomela criticized Gilbert's plural subject theory arguing that it is circular and Searle's argumentation of *we-intentions* as underdeveloped. His own proposal – based on *I-mode/we-mode* of sociability that takes joint intention, interdependent member intentions (*we-intentions*) are expressible by "we will do x together" – was, in turn, also criticized as circular (Schweikard & Bernhard Schmid, 2021). Further, even among those who agree that collectives can be the subject of intentional state ascription, there is manifest dissent: Gilbert (1989) and Tollefsen (2002, 2015) argue that it is appropriate to attribute a range of intentional states including beliefs to groups. Others, Tuomela (2004) and Wray (2001), disagree with this position as groups, in their view, can accept propositions but cannot be believers.

From this discussion, it sounds as if all proposals that stem from philosophical explanations perhaps leave us with more questions than answers (Weir, 2014), which may also apply to general approaches to individualistic intention within pragmatics, mostly stemming from a philosophy of language tradition. The role of intentionality in interpersonal communication has proven to be difficult to ascertain or agree upon, and group intentionality is certainly not an unproblematic notion either. However, the post-hoc reconstruction of intentionality via inferences and attributions is key in communication, be it interpersonal or intergroup in nature. Therefore, understanding groupness and the attribution of goals and intentions to groups are essential for humans and, not surprisingly, they have played a major role in the development of the species' social cognition (Tomasello & Rakoczy, 2003).

Certainly, knowledge about groups carries important and, sometimes, vital information and impacts attitudes and behaviors (ingroup bias, implicit bias, moral obligations); therefore, it seems essential for humans to be able to categorize others as non/members. Apparently, this is something that children as young as 3 can easily do, using mutual intentions (i.e., the general agreement of individuals that they belong to a group, Noyes & Dunham, 2017: 34) as a guiding principle, closely connected to perceived common goals (Straka et al., 2021). Once groups are constituted socially, children seem strongly inclined to believe that groupness sanctions specific ways of relating and carries with it patterns of behavior, association, and moral obligations (Noyes & Dunham, 2017: 141).

Thus, how people are transformed from a random collection of individuals into a group, a social unit, oriented to joint action is, according to Jankovic and Ludwig (2017: 1–2) *the way they think* about what they are doing together; this way of thinking constitutes the focus of study of collective intentionality[3] (CI) which can be defined as:

---

[3] It is important to point out that intentionality is not limited to intentions, which are a propositional attitude directed at actions. Intentionality "encompasses all the propositional attitudes – believing, desiring, fearing, hoping, wishing, doubting … as well as perceiving … imagining … and

> The conceptual and psychological features of joint or shared actions and attitudes and their implications for the nature of social groups and their functioning. Collective intentionality subsumes the study of collective action, responsibility, reasoning, thought, intention, emotion, phenomenology, decision-making, knowledge, trust, rationality, cooperation, competition ... as well as how these underpin social practices, organizations, conventions, institutions, and ontology.

The authors see CI as crucial to understanding the nature and structure of social reality. In this they coincide, among many others, with Tomasello and Rakoczy (2003), Tomasello et al. (2012), and Straka et al. (2021) who claim that CI is what makes human cognition unique. More specifically, Tomasello and Rakoczy (2003: 123, 143) argue that CI related skills underlie children's cultural learning and linguistic communication and enable the comprehension of cultural institutions based on collective beliefs and practices. This is important as CI is, therefore, seen as the foundation for social norms, which emanate not from individual but group opinion. As a result, conforming to social norms displays group identity. In the same way not abiding by them signals disdain for the group. That is why, as is the case with *CC*, "punishment for the laggard needs to be by the group as whole – so that when an individual enforces a social norm, she is doing so, in effect, as an emissary of the group as whole" (Tomasello et al., 2012: 683). The norms that define the group and its goals and assign roles to its members, that is, the group's CI, are in turn internalized by those members, according to Tomasello (2018: 74) as "'an objective morality'[4] in which everyone knew immediately the difference between right and wrong as determined by the group's set of cultural practices."

These claims are consequential, not only for this Element and the understanding of *cancelation* practices, but also for pragmatics. Norms, the quintessential pillars of research in many pragmatic subfields ((im)politeness among them) are the outcome of groups' collective intentionality. Therefore, a pragmatics/(im) politeness of intergroup communication needs to incorporate (social) identity and collective intentionality as key theoretical tenets. Social identity – an individual's cognitive, moral, and emotional connection with a broader community, category, practice, and institution (Polletta & Jasper, 2001) – is essentially connected to collective intentionality and both are fundamental to understanding the type of collective mobilization involved in *cancelation*.

---

emotions directed at objects and events (e.g., being angry at a perceived slight) (Jankovic & Ludwig, 2017: 1).

[4] Objective morality refers to the conceptualization of morality as universal, not up for interpretation. An objective morality of "right and wrong" is the last stage, according to Tomasello (2018), of the evolution of modern human morality. This stage is preceded by self-interest (tied to individual intentionality) and "a second person morality", that is, *me* has to be subordinated to *we*, keyed to joint intentionality.

This incorporation is not complicated if one takes a discursive approach to pragmatics/(im)politeness). Indeed, as the field underwent a discursive turn (Barron & Schneider, 2014; Locher & Watts, 2005), identity gained prominence. This is unsurprising as, according to discourse theorists (Fairclough, 2003; Gee, 2005), the construction of individual/social(group) identity is at the core of discourses, and the latter fundamentally involves collective intentionality. From this perspective, there are no apparent obstacles for pragmatics to deal with interpersonal *and* intergroup communication. In addition, as will be discussed, discourse pragmatics pays close attention to the meso-level, the level of group practices.

2.2 A Discursive Pragmatics

To tackle pragmatic phenomena, we need to ground their study in a model that includes the three levels of sociological enquiry, accounts for the interconnections among them, and offers scholars well-developed meso-level units that can tease out the role context plays in – for instance – assessments of (im)politeness (Garcés-Conejos Blitvich, 2010c, 2013).

Traditionally, three (interconnected) levels of enquiry have been identified/ applied: macro/meso/micro. Used extensively in many disciplines, what exactly they refer to is, somewhat, specific to each. In sociolinguistics/discourse analysis, macro refers to belief systems, ideologies, social structure, and institutions; meso units of communication are employed by groups and communities of practice, such as specific types of discourse or genres; whereas micro refers to specific, local interactions among participants with special attention to the syntactic, interactional, phonological, or lexical resources deployed.

In a recent discussion, Garcés-Conejos Blitvich and Sifianou (2019) argued that (im)politeness research had mostly focused on the macro/micro-levels without much regard to the essential, mediating role of the meso-level (but see Culpeper, 2021 among other publications). In addition, the shortcomings of some meso-level units of analysis commonly used in (im)politeness research, such as frames, communities of practice, and activity types, were considered. A way forward was proposed: these limitations could be assuaged by resorting to well-established, tripartite discourse models such as that proposed by Fairclough (2003)[5] and to genre as a key meso unit of analysis.

Relevant to this conversation is the fact that the starting point, as it were, of Fairclough's model is a rebuke of Bourdieu's views. For Fairclough, a key

---

[5] Please, note that although Fairclough applied his model mostly to work on Critical Discourse Analysis (CDA) this does not mean that his model is CDA based or oriented. It can be applied to a non-critical, descriptive analyses.

omission of Bourdieu's model is the lack of attention to the meso-level. As an example, when discussing political discourse, Fairclough argues that politicians never articulate political discourse in its pure form: political discourse is always situated, always shaped by genres (presidential speeches, press conferences, debates, etc.). In contrast, genre (meso-level) notions play a fundamental role in Fairclough's account of language social practices, that is, orders of discourse. Orders of discourse are defined as "the social organization and control of linguistic variation" (2003: 24). As shown in Figure 1, the way discourse figures in a social practice is thus threefold: discourses (ways of representing), genres (ways of acting, inter-acting discoursally), and styles (ways of being).

The term "discourse" is here used in two ways: (i) as an abstract noun referring to language and other kinds of semiosis as elements of social life, (ii) as a count noun referring to ways of representing a part of the world – for example, the discourse of the alt-right in the USA. Styles, in turn, refer to the role of language, along with nonverbal semiotic modes, in creating particular social or individual identities. Fairclough sees these three elements of meaning as dialectically related, each of them internalizing the others. In Fairclough's (2003: 29) words: "particular representations (discourses) may be enacted in particular ways of Acting and Relating (genres) and inculcated in particular ways of Identifying (Styles)." More specifically, style refers to "the different ways in which individuals talk in different situations to enact different identities" (Jones & Themistocleous, 2022: 135; see also Coupland, 2010). Discourses, genres, and styles are durable and stable, but they are also in constant flux. At the style level, agents are carriers, as it were, of discourse/ genres. However, they do not merely reproduce them, by constructing recognizable identities, but can reinterpret/reinvent them in a way, that if constant and shared, may significantly alter the genre and, in turn, the discourse.

Therefore, the model includes the three levels of sociological description (discourse/macro, genre/meso, style/micro) and, importantly, sees them as

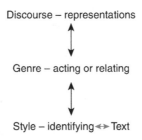

Figure 1 Discourse in social practice.

dialectically related in the sense that not only the macro/meso-levels have an impact on the micro-level, but that changes in the micro-level can alter genres and ultimately discourses. For example, the eruption of *CC's*, a macro-level phenomenon, second wave has substantially altered the micro-level realization of *cancelation* and the spaces in which it is conducted (Section 6).

In a more recent reformulation, Fairclough (2004: 381–382) added another key element to his model: that is, *texts,* "[g]enres, discourses and styles are realized in features of textual meaning." Genres situate discourses, but they are still abstractions (we have a socially acquired sense and expectations of what a lecture or health care encounter are). However, genres themselves are *instantiated in texts*: the socially situated, individually/collectively negotiated instantiations of genres.

As Fairclough (2004: 229) argues "[t]exts are the situational interactional accomplishments of social agents whose agency is, however, enabled and constrained by social structures and social practices." For example, ideologies, such as how classes should be taught, are part of our representation of Education Discourse. For its part, Education Discourse is situated in different genres, a lecture, for instance. The way a professor delivers an actual lecture will be instantiated in a *text* that will reflect the discourse and the genre but will uniquely be shaped by the professor's and the students' styles and their agencies. Thus, although text (as in text linguistics) was initially an attempt to extend grammatical principles beyond the sentence, nowadays it is "widely defined as an empirical communicative event given through human communication rather than specified by a formal theory" (de Beaugrande, 2011: 290). Consequently, discursive pragmatics' analytic focus – and the study of (im)politeness anchored therein – is the (written or spoken) *text*.

Going back to the model being discussed, Pennycook (2010), like Fairclough, acknowledged the centrality of genre in models of communication (see also Blommaert 2008, 2017a) and – to move practice theory forward – proposed to reconceptualize discourse/genre/style as practices:

> discourse, genre and style, when viewed in terms of practice, direct our attention to different ways in which we achieve social life through language: we construct realities through discursive practices, from temporary regularities to get things done through generic practices and perform social meanings with different effects through stylistic practices. (Pennycook, 2010: 122)

The dialectic relationship between Fairclough's three levels is crucial. In particular, genre and style exemplify the dual nature of practice which is:

> not reducible to individual activity nor to socially or ideologically determined behavior ... As Kemmis (2009) suggests ... practices refigure the actions of

particular actors ... these arrangements of sayings, doing, set-ups and relationships are not individual attributes but rather a set of organizing and
mediating conditions that render activity coherent. (Pennycook, 2010: 28)

This coincides with Garfinkel's (2002) view that it is practices, not individuals, that constitute the essential foundations of social structure and is very
relevant for the present discussion: some genre practices – such as demonstra-
tions, boycotts, group exclusion, *cancelation*, are collective in nature and
cannot be reduced to the individual level. In addition, the rest of genre
practices (although not necessarily collective as in the other examples) such
as, for instance, a service encounter, also involve two salient social identities
(service/provider and customer, of course, colored by individual styles) that
cannot be understood unless with reference to a group and thus constitute
intergroup communication.

Taking a discursive approach and genre practices as a meso-level unit allows
us to circumvent any potential problems regarding analyzing collective/inter-
group-based practices, as they are part and parcel of generic expectations and
constraints. Further, a discursive approach allows us to conceptualize how
discourses are often not realized by just one genre practice but, as with *CC*,
by a genre ecology (multiple genres working together to achieve the same end)
brought together contingently for each case of *cancelation* (Section 5). In the
next sections, I pay detailed attention to the meso-level as the level of genres
practices and the level of groups, respectively.

2.2.1 Genres and the Meso-Level

As emphasized throughout this Element, meso-level practices are essentially
related to groups and, thus, merge in well with the intergroup perspective
advocated here. In taking this step, as pragmatics becomes discourse-centered,
pragmaticians of different persuasions can draw interdisciplinarily from linguistic and rhetoric fields that have made meso-level practices one of their main
objects of research, such as Systemic Functional Linguistics, English for
Specific Purposes (ESP), and Rhetorical Genre Studies.

It is the last two approaches I mostly draw from in my own understanding of
genre. Regarding the first, in its foundational paper, Miller (1984) approached
genre as social action and defined genres as "typified rhetorical actions" that
respond to recurring situations and become instantiated in groups' behaviors.
Miller argued that "a rhetorical sound definition of genre must be centered not
on the substance or the form of discourse, but on the action, it is used to
accomplish" (151), which – in Miller's view – makes them pragmatic in nature.
Bazerman (1997: 19), a key contributor to this approach, summarizes it well:

> Genres are not just forms. Genres are forms of life, ways of being. They are frames for social action. They are environments for learning. They are locations within which meaning is constructed. Genres shape the thoughts we form and the communications by which we interact. Genres are the familiar places we go to create intelligible communicative action with each other and the guideposts we use to explore the unfamiliar.

Further, genres are stabilized-for-now but constantly-in-flux sites of social and ideological action (Berkenkotter & Huckin, 1993) and thus *recognizable* by members of communities. As Bazerman (1994: 100) pointed out, "[w]ithout a shared sense of genre, others would not know what kind of thing we are doing." Importantly, as the meso-level realization of discourses, genres open certain positions, roles, and relationships, since identity is always at the core of discourses/genres (Bazerman, 1994; Blommaert, 2017a; Fairclough, 2003; Gee, 2005). Relevant to our discussion, knowledge of genres through socialization practices includes rhetorical expertise, dynamic knowledge of processes and audience's expectations (regarding norms of behavior, for instance) (Tardy, 2009)

Miller (2015), when pondering on the influence of her foundational views, argued that genre continues to be a useful concept because it connects our experiences to our sense of the past and the future, makes recurrent patterns significant, and very importantly for this Element, it characterizes communities by offering modes of engagement through joint action and uptake.[6]

Within ESP, one of the most influential definitions of genre was provided by Swales (1990: 58): "A genre comprises a class of communicative events, the members of which share some set of communicative purposes. These purposes are recognized by the expert members of the parent discourse community, and thereby constitute the rationale for the genre." Swales' model is referred to as the three-level genre model and provides a useful template for the actual analysis of genres.

Communicative purpose/goal emerges as the main rationale for the genre and triggers a move structure. Moves are understood as discoursal or rhetorical units that perform a coherent communicative function in a written or spoken discourse (Swales, 2004: 228), where some moves are essential/obligatory and others are nonobligatory. For instance, in resumes, one is expected to include a part (move) on education and another on professional experience, whereas a move on hobbies is not necessarily expected. For their part, rhetorical strategies refer to the different semiotic modes (lexico-grammatical structures, jargon, layout, font, register, among others) used at the micro-level to realize each move

---

[6] "Uptake" is the illocutionary response elicited by particular situations.

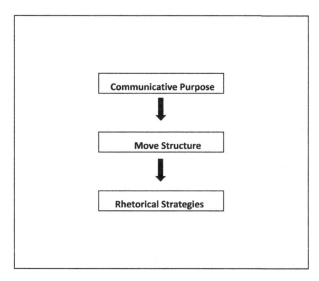

Figure 2 Swales' model.

and carry out the general purpose of the genre, and are, therefore, audience-designed. To continue with the same example, a resume follows a well-established and recognizable layout and uses professional-looking fonts; it should be formal in register, use field-related jargon, be short (circa two pages for corporate jobs), and so on In this respect, as mentioned, genres are stabilized for now and socio-rhetorical; therefore, move structure and rhetorical strategies are also in flux as communities' conventions and expectations change or influential trailblazers fundamentally alter the genre in a bottom-up fashion.

Relatedly, the advent of digital technologies partly changed, among many others, our conceptualization of texts and genres, as traversals facilitated by hyperlinks created significantly different expectations regarding the finiteness of texts and the high hybridization of genres (Bhatia, 2015; Lemke, 2002). Although mentioned in relation to digital mediation, as Bhatia (2015) argued, hybridization is a constant across genres, despite scholarship having tended to focus on "pure" genres. For instance, antitobacco bills merge and enact legal and health discourses. However, genres do not only merge and influence one another, they relate to each other in a myriad of other ways, as it is not often the case that a given activity can be carried out by just one single genre. Note how a political campaign or a college application involve many genres practices coming together to achieve a specific goal: being (re)elected and being (re) admitted, respectively; those genre practices include, to name a few, from phone calls and letters to potential voters/donors, flyers, rallies, fundraisers, and so on, in the case of campaigns, and application forms, statements of purpose, official transcripts, letters of recommendation, meetings with academic advisors and finance counselors, and so on in the case of applications.

As a result, scholars have devised conceptualizations regarding how genres come together, such as in genre sets (full range of the kind of texts that one person uses to fill out one side of a multiple-person interactions, Bazerman, 1994), genre systems ("interrelated genres that interact with each other in specific settings," Bazerman, 1994: 97), genre repertoires ("The set of genres that are routinely enacted by the members of a community," Orlikowski & Yates, 1994: 542), genre sequences (a similar concept to genre systems, Swales, 2004), genre colonies (a term developed to describe how genres move from one activity system to another to create new clusters of genres, Bhatia, 2002), and genre ecologies (a contingent, interacting, interdependent system or network of genres, as distinct from a series of genres with a specifically sequential series of uptake, Spinuzzi & Zachry, 2000).[7]

It is the last concept, genre ecologies, that I find particularly useful. Applying this model to the data, I will argue that *cancelation* is carried out by complex genre ecologies (Section 5.2).

3 Groups and the Meso-Level

Out of the three sociological levels of analysis described and discussed in Section 2.2, the meso-level has been one of the most debated and problematized dimensions of social theory and sociology (Serpa & Ferreira, 2019). What scholars agree on is that social order is embodied in patterns of social relationships, occurring in different domains and scales, and seen "in the similarities of individual behaviors as in the *regularities of encounters between human agents*, in *the establishment of groups* and organizations as in the functioning of institutions and in the distribution of social resources" (my emphasis, Pires, 2012: 40).

Regarding groups, as Fine (2012: 159) points out, "A focus on the groups – the meso-level of analysis – enriches both structural and interactional approaches, stressing shared and ongoing meaning. Groups constitute social order, just as groups themselves are constituted by that order." More recently, Fine and Hallett (2014) argued that groups and the meso-level not only mediate the micro and the meso-levels, but that the meso-level has semi-autonomous properties and dynamics that shape everyday life. These dynamics can be related to five processes crucially related to groups by Harrington and Fine (2000) namely, controlling, contesting, organizing, representing, and allocating, some of which, as we will discuss (Section 6), are of key to the present analysis. These processes, according to the authors, show that groups are the locus of

---

[7] See Spinuzzi (2004) for a detailed comparison of genre assemblages.

social control and social change. What is clear is that through the study of groups, we can concentrate, among others, on social identity, collective intentionality, collective action via engagement in genre practices, and group culture, which are key to the understanding of *CC* and the practice of *cancelation*, which aims to effect both social control and social change (Garcés-Conejos Blitvich, 2022a, 2022b).

As discussed, groups are essential to cognition and to society (Section 2.1.3). Not surprisingly, group research has a long trajectory (starting in the 1850s and getting established in 1930s*)* and has been approached from a variety of disciplines (psychology, sociology, anthropology, philosophy, organizational science, and education, to name a few (Gençer, 2019*)*. Providing a definition of group has proven not to be easy, as it may overlap with that of network, community, or organization (Fine, 2012: 172). Fine (2012: 160) claims that they are an "aggregation of persons that is characterized by shared place, common identity, collective culture, and social relations." To be a group, a crowd should have common objectives, norms, and share a feeling of groupness (Gençer, 2019). In addition, it has been argued that *emotional commitment* to a group and its local culture sets the standards for action that shape the group and project this action outward (Lawler, 1992). Tying groups to their meso-level practices, Garfinkel (2002) does not define groups on the bases of demographic characteristics, kinship relations, or cultural practices/beliefs held by people across time, space, and political connections. Instead, groups are defined by Garfinkel by the practices that constitute their membership. Therefore, to constitute a group a set of persons needs to be mutually engaged in enacting a situated practice in a way that said practices define the pertinent social identities and interactional possibilities for all of those involved – thereby constituting them as recognizable and competent members.

Further, scholarship has provided different classifications of groups, among others: primary/secondary groups, based on contact; ingroup/outgroup, based on identification; formal/informal groups, based on rules/regulations; voluntary/involuntary based on choice of membership; institutional/non/institutional; temporary and permanent; un-social, pseudo-social, anti-social, and pro-social groups based on relation to society; large/small in relation to size (see Gençer, 2019, for a discussion).

Significantly for this Element, related research (Blommaert, 2017a, 2017b) has also distinguished, between "*thick*" groups – that is, (i) traditional demographic categories (such as race, gender, ethnicity, nation, class, caste, family, profession, and religion) and (ii) tight-knit, established networks in which people share many norms, values and collective representations – and "*light*" groups, or less conspicuous forms of relationship and social interaction (such as those observed by Goffman, 1961) which involve moments of tight but temporary groupness (Blommaert, 2017b). Light groups, although also common offline, are closely related to online interactions – such as those that form around particular configurations of communicative resources and social practices: from memes to conspiracy theories, to online platform challenges – and to what has been labeled the "networked society" (Castells, 1996) which has substantially altered the essence and understanding of groups, as they cannot be contained within traditional boundaries (Appadurai, 1996). I will return to this point in more detail in the next section.

Although thick groups have traditionally received the bulk of academic attention, for most people, in "daily lived experience membership in 'light' communities prevails over that of 'thick' communities" (Blommaert, 2017a: 50). Therefore, understanding contemporary forms of social cohesion requires an awareness of the key role of light communities. It is important to consider, however, that the thick/light distinction should be taken as a cline, rather than discreet categories. In this respect, Fine (2012: 65) claims that sociability networks, that is, light interaction, can evolve into a thick form of community when members collaborate toward a common goal. Similarly, Blommaert (2017a) concurred that "light" communities can exhibit many features habitually ascribed to "thick" communities. For instance, light communities can display a heavy quality due to the passion, zeal, and shared outrage/violence that those involved in them can express.

It can be argued that this is the case of the light groups that assemble for *cancelation* pursuits (referred to as mobs or social justice activists, depending on ideological positioning, Romano, 2021). The shared goals of expressing outrage, enacting social regulation, and denouncing, exposing, and making *cancelees* face consequences for their actions (Garcés-Conejos Blitvich, 2022b), as we will see, give the group entitativity (i.e., how much a group or collective is perceived by others as an actual entity with cohesion, coherence, and internal organization, rather than just a collection of separate individuals) and make it coalesce around recognizable genre practices – *cancelation*, Sections 5 and 6 – that co-constitute the group identity. Further, these light groups can mesh with other more established thick groups (as in the case of *cancelation* which is a prime example of the on/offline nexus of post digital societies and involves both on- and off-line practices, Section 5) to carry out powerful types of activism that, in some cases, have been likened to "revolutionary action" (Costea, 2017).

Regardless of its thickness/lightness, a group's identity will be closely tied to the genre practices it engages in – that is, a group is what a group does (Angouri, 2015: 325), *cancelation* in the case here under scrutiny. As

Blommaert (2017a: 40–45) has argued regarding his genre theory of social action, "[c]ommunicative practice is always and invariably an act of identity [and] identity work is . . . genre based." Social actors, that is, group members, are ephemeral (they pass on, may leave the group and join others, etc.) but iterative group-associated practices, although always in flux – and thus also creative, in the sense that they can deviate from genre templates – tend to remain and offer the necessary continuity and recognizability (Blommaert et al., 2018; Garfinkel, 2002) for the group to perpetuate itself. As Rawls (2005) argued, it is situations that afford the appearance of individuals and not the other way around. In other words, practices/actions generate those who are involved in them.

What is also key to this discussion is how groups (either thick or light) become agents. As with other aspects of group research, it is mostly thick groups that have been seen as constituting group agents, that is, a group organized to have group-level representation and motivation and the capacity to act on their basis. Group agents – such as several of the ones that participated in the three *cancelations* here under scrutiny, for instance, NBC (National Broadcasting Corporation), ESPN (Entertainment and Sports Programming Network), and the House of Representatives – have systems in place to process individual voices, opinions, and so on, into a singular voice (voting, decision hierarchies, etc.). Importantly, the beliefs, decisions, and actions we attribute to the group are not reducible to the beliefs of individuals (List & Pettit, 2011; see Section 2.1.3 for a discussion of non-reductive views).

However, can light groups become group agents? I will argue that they can, albeit in different ways from thick groups. What makes the two processes similar is the claiming of certain social identities, the establishment of common goals, emotional investment, and the involvement in collective action to achieve said goals. In the case of the light groups that engage in online *cancelation*, online spaces play a key role in facilitating group entitativity and agency.

3.1 Groups and Online Spaces

In Section 4, the situatedness and historical aspects of *CC* will be scrutinized; here, the focus will be on the spaces where online *cancelation* takes place, and which facilitate those light groups involved in the practice to become group agents. Space emerges as key both for this Element and groups in general. Relevant for this analysis is the concept of *scenes*, that is, places in which individuals with similar interests gather with the expectation of finding like-minded others and engaging in shared action (Fine, 2012). The *scenes* of the twenty-first century are often mediated digitally.

Indeed, as mentioned, digital communication was instrumental in establishing a networked society (Castells, 1996; Papacharissi, 2011) by greatly facilitating the creation of endless types of groupings and, in doing so, it was also conducive to the problematization of traditional concepts such as *group, community,* and social *network.* In this respect, translocality, among others, has fundamentally shifted how groupness emerges online, as it is no longer predicated on strong and lasting ties anchored in shared bodies of knowledge or facilitated by temporal or spatial co-presence (Varis & van Nuenen, 2017). Similarly, it has been argued that individualization is a key feature of global connectivity; it assumes that "digital communication networks have transformed people's social relationships from hierarchical, arranged, stable, tightly, and densely bounded groups to more fluid, dispersed, episodic, and less bounded relationships … global networked audiences are active agents who can make free choices based on their own interests, preferences, and affiliations" (Li & Jung, 2018: 4). Alternative concepts: *online affinity spaces* (Gee, 2005), *ambient affiliation* (Zappavigna, 2014), *conviviality* (Blommaert & Varis, 2015) were proposed to capture the light nature of online groupness, the often-limited requirements for group affiliation (shared activities, interests, and common goals) and participation (Blommaert, 2017a).

Often, these groupings have been described as communities of knowledge or epistemic oriented communities, although eudaimonic (i.e., pertains to the personal feelings linked with eudaimonia, or striving for human excellence through virtuous living) social variables such as the establishment/maintenance of social relationships of conviviality, group cohesion, desire for happiness, self-efficacy, etc. have been seen as facilitating the formation of that collective knowledge (Blommaert, 2017a; Vähämaa, 2013). Scholars have also devoted significant attention to hashtag/memic activism and the groups that are temporarily or more permanently united via the common use of a hashtag or the continuous permutation and recontextualization of memes (see Blommaert, 2017b; Bonilla & Rosa, 2015; Zeng & Abidin, 2021). Clearly, ambient affiliation, online affinity spaces are not traditional groups, but a sense of community is evident in the different and often frequent ways in which online users attempt to reach and connect with each other.

Cyberspace does offer a multitude of translocal digital spaces where like-minded individuals engage in different types of group-shared action. Digital spaces are thus very facilitative of group formations and provide a window into how people behave as members of groups, that is, when their social identity is salient, and engage in intergroup communication. Intergroup communication is pervasive online since digital environments foster *deindividuation.* Although initial deindividuation models related it to antinormative conduct, other approaches (as the SIDE, Social Identity Model of Deindividuation Effects, model, based on Social Identity theory; Reicher et al., 1995) have argued that deindividuation, in digital environments does not necessarily foster deregulation of social behavior but increases the saliency of social identity and group-associated social norms, which are key to intergroup communication. In this sense, often in technologically mediated practices, individuals' personal characteristics must be set aside in order to participate successfully (Rawls, 2005).

It is important to consider that the positive connotations of affiliation, affinity, and conviviality may predispose one to think of online communities as rapport-based groupings, engaging in playfulness and other ludic activities (Blommaert, 2017b) devoid of any intra/inter manifestations of conflict. However, this is not always the case (see Blommaert, 2017c; Garcés Conejos Blitvich, 2021, 2022a, 2022b), as not infrequently groups will assemble online very purposefully to turn some scenes into the *tyrannical spaces* (Andrews & Chen, 2006) where *cancelation* takes place.

CC – more specifically in its first wave (Section 4.2) – was understood as a way to challenge and hold accountable powerful individuals who had been perceived as acting immorally and, concurrently, to empower traditionally disenfranchised groups by giving them a voice. Collective protest and boycott were unprecedentedly facilitated by massive access to online, public spaces. In this sense, online spaces can be likened, with a few caveats, to "free spaces." According to Rao and Dutta (2012), free spaces are arenas – in organizations and societies – shielded from the control of elites which promote collective empowerment and intense emotion and trigger collective identities, enabling individuals to engage in collective action. Arguing that more attention needs to be paid to how protest spaces themselves shape interaction and strategies therein, Au (2017) reconceptualized online spaces as "free spaces" and tied them to the affordances and constraints offered by digital media which enable certain types of engagement (and not others). More specifically, Au (2017: 147) claimed that online free spaces are strategic in supporting the exchange of information, mass recruitment, and the expression of (oppositional) identities (*canceler*s and *cancelee*s in this case).

Taking into consideration that most social media platforms are in the hands of powerful individuals and corporations and regulated by proprietary algorithms about whose function and impact on us we know little (Cheney-Lippold, 2017), it is hard to equate online free spaces with the initial conceptualizations of free spaces as completely shielded from the control of the elite. Nonetheless, they certainly meet the other requirements, and, notably, algorithms themselves play a role in bringing like-minded people together, and, thus, in group formation, by circulating content to people based on what they have been engaged with in the past.

This conceptualization of online free spaces as shaping interaction and facilitating the emergence of certain identities is in line with Goffman's (1963b), Scollon and Wong Scollon's (2003), and Blommaert's (2013) views on on/offline spaces as being regulative and thus historical, political, and tied to emotions; the latter is also argued by emotional geographies (Davidson et al., 2005), that is, the study of the feelings people attach to physical places (i.e., how emotions both have spatial affects and affect space). Indeed, it is due to the collective organizational/regulative/emotive power that online spaces afford that such light groupings can become group agents. It is important to note that becoming group agents is essential to then engage with other groups agents, the offline thick groups already mentioned, such as those that ultimately carry out *cancelation*. As we will see, the complex genre ecologies involved in *cancelation* (Section 5) both require and facilitate for light/thick groups to coalesce into hybrid, contingent groups, a phenomenon that has received less attention.

In view of what has just been discussed, it becomes clear that pragmatics/(im) politeness should not obviate the theoretical and empirical ramifications of intergroup communication. A complex socio-cultural, collective phenomenon such as *CC* needs to be approached from an equally complex model that allows the analyst a holistic view of its realizations at the macro/meso/micro-levels. I have proposed that Fairclough's model provides the necessary tools and complexity to tackle this task. More importantly, with its inclusion of genre practices as meso-level units, it is uniquely equipped to pay attention to intergroup communication and groups in general, as the meso-level is the level of groups, both in the sense of some genres making social identities (and thus intergroup communication) salient (e.g., a meeting between a boss and employee) and also in the sense that some genre practices cannot be fulfilled by individuals but are unavoidably collective and tied to collective intentionality. A focus on collective action, as needed in *cancelation*, implies scrutinizing how thick and light groups come together with a common goal (or set of goals) that requires the deployment of a complex, contingent genre ecology to bring it/them to fruition. Notably, online *cancelation* micro-level practices will be scrutinized to offer a rare glimpse (as they have been mostly approached from a macro-level perspective) into how light groups coalesce and turn into group agents, this being facilitated by the normativity, morality, and emotions associated with online spaces, along with their digital affordances.

Figure 3 summarizes Sections 2 and 3 and brings together Fairclough's (2003) discourse in social practice model and the social phenomenon here under scrutiny: *CC*.

By paying close attention to *CC* as a socio-cultural phenomenon and the complexities of three cases of *cancelation* involving: Congresswoman Liz

Discourses - Representations – **Macro-level** – *Cancel Culture*

Genres – Acting/relating – **Meso-level** – *Cancelation*- Genre ecologies involved in Cheney's, DeGeneres', & Nichols' *cancelation*s. Out of these ecologies, the genre of user-generated comments was selected for micro-level analysis.

Styles – Identifying ⟵━━━⟶ Texts - **Micro-level** – **User-generated comments** (in *CC* corpus)

Figure 3 Summary.

Cheney, comedian Ellen DeGeneres', and sports commentator Rachel Nichols – the next part of this Element seeks to answer the following research questions:

RQ1 – How can *CC* be conceptualized at the macro-level?

RQ2 – What genre, meso-level, practices are involved in *cancelation*?

RQ3 – How is *cancelation* realized at the micro-level? (with a focus on online practices)

RQ 3.1 – How do the micro-level resources used contribute to the light groups involved in *cancelation* becoming agents?

The methodology described below was devised to help answer these questions. Please note that, as mentioned in the introduction and for ease of reading, the complex methodology applied to the three levels under analysis has been split into three sections (4.1, 5.1, and 6.1) immediately preceding each analytic level. After tackling *CC* as a sociocultural phenomenon, Section 4.3 presents an overview of the three cases of *cancelation* to further contextualize the meso and micro analyses, which are then detailed.

4 Macro-Level Analysis: *Cancel Culture* as a Big C Conversation

4.1 Methods: Macro-Level Analysis

This segment of the analysis addresses RQ1, which probes how *CC* can be conceptualized at the macro-level. More specifically, it seeks to understand the historical and political events that shaped its development and distribution in the USA, how it may vary across different social or cultural groups, how it is influenced and evaluated depending on the different cultural values and beliefs held, and how it may reflect or challenge existing social structures or power relations. In sum, by answering these questions, a macro-level analysis can lead to a broader understanding of a particular phenomenon and its place in history, culture, or society. More specifically from a pragmatic perspective, this type of analysis provides insights into the ways in which communicative behavior is shaped by larger socio-cultural factors.

To understand macro societal phenomena, analyses involve a combination of historical and archival research. Further, macro analyses often comprise statistics that span long periods and construct data sets that show how social systems and the relationships within them have evolved over time to produce contemporary society.

For this part, as a US resident, I have followed *CC* closely since 2018, when it was starting to be mentioned along other related terms such as *Outrage Culture* and *Call out Culture* and collected a significant amount of commentary both from reputable legacy media and from online sources, such as YouTube channels, that explained what, at the time, was not a mainstream concept. *CC* became an umbrella term for different forms of public outrage between 2020 and 2021 (per Google Trends) and related academic research started to emerge, which I also compiled and studied. With significant exceptions (Bouvier, 2020, among others), most related research has looked at *CC* from a macro-level perspective. In that respect, I was able to draw from quite a prolific body of work despite the novelty of the topic.

Interesting, in the sense of providing archival research on the phenomenon, were Barnhizer's (2021) study, which documents 600 cases of individuals that were canceled in the USA, Duchi's (2021) qualitative analysis of 103 online articles and think pieces debating *CC*, and the work by Vogels et al. (2021), for the Pew Research Center, that offers detailed statistics regarding how widespread the term *CC* is and how it is understood by different social groups in the USA, with special emphasis on political persuasion. Further, from a discourse studies perspective, I drew insights from Fairclough (2003) and Gee (2014). A macro-level understanding of *CC* is presented in the next section.

4.2 Results of the Macro-level Analysis: Understanding of CC as a Big C Conversation

A concept related to the macro-level is that of Big C Conversation. Big C Conversations (Gee, 2014) help us understand *CC*, as in a short span, *CC* became one. Ng (2020: 623) defined *CC* as "the withdrawal of any kind of support (viewership, social media follows, purchases of products endorsed by the person, etc.) from those who are assessed to have said or done something unacceptable or highly problematic, generally from a social justice perspective especially alert to sexism, heterosexism, homophobia, racism, bullying and related issues." Adding ethnocentrism, antisemitism, islamophobia, and ageism, Norris (2023) emphasizes perceptions of moral offense as the common denominator among triggers. For its part, a Big C Conversation (Gee, 2014) refers to the public debates about the Discourses (affirmative action, abortion rights, feminism, race, etc.) that make up society and are, thus, all around us in the media and our interactions with others. In these types of debates, everyone involved generally has a good sense of what the sides are and what sorts of people tend to be on each side. That certainly would seem to be the case with *CC* which has become a sub-set of the Culture Wars, that is, the cultural divide "between those who welcome or oppose liberal value change" (Kaufmann, 2022: 774)

Regarding its inception, it is claimed that *cancel* has its roots in a 1980 slang term meaning to break up with somebody (Vogels et al., 2021), others relate it to a 1981 single "Your love is canceled" and point to a misogynistic joke in the movie *New Jack City* for expanding canceling to a whole individual (Romano, 2020, 2021). *Cancel* had been used by queer communities of color (Clark, 2020), in ways that resonated with the civil rights boycotts of the 1950s and 1960s (Romano, 2020), to refer to the withdrawal of support and attention from those (usually celebrities) whose behavior was perceived to be problematic, offensive, or to have transgressed against group norms. Later (circa 2014) the term was popularized through Black Twitter. However, *CC* and its associated practices, that is, *cancelation*, were not widely known outside the initial contexts of use until 2019 and did not gain mainstream notoriety until 2020 and 2021.[8] Vogels et al. (2021) showed how in September 2020, 44% of Americans had heard a fair amount about *CC*. More recently, in 2022, that number had gone up to 61% (Vogels, 2022).

Originally, *CC* was seen as a tool of empowerment for those black (and other disenfranchised) communities that engaged in it, a way to exercise their power to ignore the powerful (Romano, 2021), participate in public debates about morality (Mueller, 2021), and, thus, to criticize systemic inequality rather than an attack on individual transgressions (Clark, 2020: 89). As it expanded, however, *CC* underwent a pejoration process by being conflated with some of its own tools (public shaming) and other related trends such as *Call out Culture*, which resulted in the two phenomena being generically referred as *Outrage Culture* (Clark, 2020; Romano, 2021). However, public shaming

---

[8] Per google trends https://trends.google.com/trends/explore?date=2017-02-11%202022-03-11&geo=US&q=Cancel%20culture,%22woke%20culture%22.

    Romano (2021), however, argues that CC started trickling into mainstream conversations in 2014.

(although frequently used in its mediated form in *CC*) has been a common practice in Western societies and was often used to punish deviants before legal systems were in place (Reichl, 2019). For its part, *Call out Culture*, pointing out a problem and going after the individual who caused it, also pre-dates *CC* and is related to the early 2010s Tumblr callout blogs (Romano, 2019).

There is no denying that *CC* is perceived as "real." Where lay individuals, the mainstream media, and scholars disagree on is whether it should be seen either as an expression of agency, attempting to hold transgressors accountable, or as an unjust, silencing weapon. In a voluminous account of 600 cases that involved *CC*, Barnhizer (2021: 3) contended:

> A "small but intransigent minority" is consuming us. They are the "*Cancelers*" ... The existence and harm of *CC* is real. *CC* is bad. Although it purports to be for equality racial justice and harmony, *CC* is fundamentally racist ... *CC* is a powerful strategy of suppression being imposed on the American people by much of the nation's media, Internet platforms, dominant social media actors, impassioned activists, and cold-hearted politicians.

Similar thoughts were express in "A Letter on Justice and Open Debate,"[9] published in Harper's Magazine in July 2020 and signed by over 150 writers, academics, and intellectuals. The letter, stating concerns about a perceived growing intolerance for diverse opinions and a chilling effect on free speech and open debate in society, highlighted the dangers of *CC* and "the intolerant climate that has set in on all sides." It argued that the free exchange of ideas is essential to a healthy democracy and that the only way to counter bad ones is through open discussion and criticism. It also called attention to the impact that *CC* and online shaming can have on individuals' lives and careers and warned against the use of these tactics to silence dissenting voices.

On the other side of the Big C Conversation, we find scholars like Clark (2020: 89), who view things rather differently, as can be gleaned from the following:

> Politicians, pundits, celebrities, academics, and everyday people have narrativized being canceled into a moral panic akin to actual harm ... associating it with an unfounded fear of censorship and silencing, but being canceled – a designation, it should be noted, usually reserved for celebrities, brands, and otherwise out-of-reach figures – should be read as a last-ditch appeal for justice.

Indeed, it seems that *CC* (as almost everything of import) has undergone, at face value, political polarization in the context of the USA. Some (Fahey et al., 2023; Romano, 2021) argue that we are now experiencing a "second wave" of *CC*

---

which is the result of it being weaponized, likened to a mob rule, by the Right. Indeed, Fahey et al. (2023) contend that the modern Republican Party (GOP)[10] has instituted *CC* as an essential element of its platform. In this respect, *CC* is often negatively invoked by Republican politicians and conservative news outlets since opposition to *CC* is seen as ideologically congruent. Among others, former President Trump, when accepting his party's nomination at the 2020 Republican convention, claimed that "The goal of *CC* is to make decent Americans live in fear of being fired, expelled, shamed, humiliated and driven from society as we know it." At the same convention, a third of designated speakers mentioned *CC* as a concerning political phenomenon. In the spring of 2021, Representative Jim Jordan (Republican, Ohio) requested a congressional investigation into, in his view, *CC*'s substantial and long-term consequences to American democracy and its constitutional framework. Regarding news outlets Fox News, a premier conservative channel, has a dedicated space on their webpage to facilitate its viewers' being on the front lines of this modern-day cultural conflict "as the fear of being canceled sweeps the country."[11]

It is mostly during this so-called second wave that the term *woke*, also having its origins in the slang of black communities and going mainstream in 2010, ended up becoming an "insult." As McWhorter (2021) describes as late as 2016, *woke*, as in *stay woke*, generally had positive connotations, and referred to being in "on a leftist take on how American society operates, especially in reference to the condition of Black America and the role of systemic racism within it." By 2020, it had become a synonym of (even a replacement for) politically correct and used as a slur "hurled at the left from the right and even from the center." As a result, there seems to be a strong association in some circles between *wokeness* and *CC*, which positions the latter as a manifestation of the former (Velasco, 2020) as the micro-analysis of the data (Section 6) clearly shows. Interesting in this respect is Governor DeSantis (Republican, Florida) who signed the Stop W.O.K.E. (Stop Wrongs Against Our Kids and Employees) Act into law in 2022 (in March 2023, the Florida's Eleventh Circuit Court of Appeals left in place a preliminary injunction blocking such act); this act seeks to restrict how conversations about race and gender take place at schools, colleges and workplaces by banning discussions that would result into making people feel "guilty" or "uncomfortable" about past wrongs, such as slavery (for a discussion on the intersections between the teaching of critical race theory and *CC*, see Kaufmann, 2022).

Despite their many protestations against *CC*, and their attributing its practices to furibund "woke, liberal mobs," it has been claimed that conservatives engage

---

[10] Grand Old Party.   [11] www.foxnews.com/category/topic/cancel-culture.

in similar *cancelation* practices when companies and organizations (such as Delta Airlines and Baseball Major League) go against the GOP's interests (for example by expressing concern about Georgia voting rights bills) (Romano, 2021); it has also been discussed that there is a Trump *CC* effect on those in his party who oppose or fail to appropriately support him, a prime example being Congresswoman Cheney. Relevantly, the claim that *CC* mostly targets conservatives seems not to be tenable, as individuals across the political spectrum have been canceled (Saint-Louis, 2021).

The divisions regarding *CC* seen in academia, politics, and the media are unsurprisingly mirrored by public opinion. In 2022, when prompted to provide a definition of *CC*, 51% of Americans familiar with the term related it to actions people take to hold others accountable, whereas 45% saw it as connected to forms of censorship such as restricting free speech or erasing history. However, out of those only 34% of Republicans/leaning Republican described it in terms of accountability compared to 65% of Democrats/leaning Democrat. Indeed, 62% of Republicans/leaning Republican also believed that *CC*-related practices tend to punish people who do not deserve it, whereas only 32% of Democrats/Leaning Democrat agreed with this statement. Concerning race, Black adults (71%) are particularly likely to equate *CC* with a culture of consequences, or a way to hold people accountable, followed by Hispanic and Asian (61% respectively) and White adults (44%). Regarding gender, women (56%) are more inclined than men (45%) to see *CC* as accountability rather than unjust punishment (Vogels, 2022; Vogels et al., 2021). These results, regarding race and gender, tie in well with *CC* being seen, as in its first wave, as the empowerment of minorities.

Mueller (2021) reached comparable conclusions when researching perceptions of *CC*. Results suggested that demanding an apology is at the heart of *CC*. However, significant differences emerged in relation to political ideology and gender: "As citizens move towards conservative political identity, their intent to demand an apology decreases ... Regarding gender traits, as respondent masculinity increases the desire to demand apologies decreases ... As liberal identity increases, their desire to 'forgive and forget' will decrease" (11). Similarly, Kaufman's (2022) – related to current issues facing the USA in relation to partisanship – showed that the calling for limits to certain forms of speech and actions associated with *CC* are a mid-rank issue overall and a leading issue for Republican voters. Cook et al. (2021), for their part, found a different correlation between engaging in *CC*-related practices and ideology; in their analysis, conservatives and non-partisans appeared to be the group more likely to engage in such practices.

It is hard to reach general conclusions based on these studies, as they all have limitations: they either rely on post hoc assessments and questionnaires, are the result of lab-created experiments, or restrict *CC* triggers to inappropriate online postings. Also, data could be reflecting changing trends in a rapidly changing phenomenon or, as Cook et al. (2021) argue, broad categories such as "American," "Democrat," "Republican" may not be useful in describing online aggression. In this respect, it is interesting to note that the percentages of both Republicans/Leaning Republican and Democrats/Leaning Democrat groups obtained in 2022 regarding those who saw *CC* as unfair punishment increased when compared to those obtained in 2020 (see Vogels et al., 2021; Vogels, 2022).

There is also considerable discussion regarding what the collective intentionality of groups engaging in *CC* may be. Since *CC* is considered, mostly across the board, as an online phenomenon research has focused almost entirely on the related groups that gather online. Nonetheless, there is also disagreement in this regard. Garcés-Conejos Blitvich (2022) found that the main goals of those who engaged in online public shaming, one of the tools of *CC*, was (i) to ostracize those who had transgressed against group norms, the *cancelees*, and expose them for what they truly are (in order to dismantle their reputation, Mueller, 2021), (ii) to make them accountable (e.g., by having them face legal or financial repercussions, see also Lewis & Christin, 2022), and (iii) to effect social regulation in the sense of pre-emptively trying to dissuade others to act in similar ways or else. This is noteworthy as psychological research on ostracism, and the motives behind it, has likened it to social control used to manage threats to a group's well-being (Wesselmann et al., 2013). In general, coercive potential and embodiment of the social order are key features of groups (Harrington & Fine, 2000; see section 2.2.3). Certainly, social control and power struggle seem to be at the core of a collective phenomenon such as *CC,* described by some as a tool to destabilize power, that is, as a power play between groups: those who used to control public discourse and newcomers to the public sphere whose presence in the debate has been facilitated by digital technologies (Clark, 2020; Romano, 2021; Thiele, 2021).

Interestingly those survey participants who, in Vogels et al. (2021), saw *CC* as unjust punishment, understood the motivations behind it as mostly silencing those who have a dissenting opinion, forcing their views on others, and trying to marginalize White voices and history. Yet, other interesting takes argue that the main goal of those engaging in *CC* is to obtain an apology (Mueller, 2021) and that polarized and cathartic responses, such as those involved in *CC*, stem from the will to reinforce group values and carry out social posturing regarding one's claimed social identity (al-Gharbi, 2022).

For the same reason stated (the fact that *CC* has mostly been considered an online phenomenon (or at least its online manifestations have received the bulk of the attention) and equated with one of its tools (i.e., online public shaming), groups carrying out *cancelation* have been described as smart mobs. These mobs are seen as coming together mostly for the goal of punishing and degrading others in the search for social justice, often through online public shaming (Lazarus, 2017). Depending on the different positions regarding *CC* discussed, mobs can be characterized in negative terms as *cyber digilantes* or *digilantes* (Juliano, 2012; Sorell, 2019; see also Citron, 2014 on the destructive nature of online mobs) but also in positive terms such as *social justice activists* or *discourse activists* (Romano, 2021; Shaw, 2012). In this Element, the more neutral *canceler* was chosen to avoid binary positionings and also to be able to refer to those participating in offline *cancelation*. Returning to mobs, creating a smart mob has been described as requiring five essential components: a desire for communication, affordable communication devices, opportunities for instantaneous communication, a shared goal, and short-time frame (Harmon & Metaxas, 2010, but see Garcés-Conejos Blitvich, 2021). A shared goal is seen as the critical component of a mob (as it also is of the genre practice/s it engages in; Section 2.2) and what distinguishes it from regular network activity. No smart mob is disbanded until its goal is achieved (Lazarus, 2017: 45); the *cancelation* of targets, in the cases here under scrutiny.

From the above, it can be gathered that a good understanding of *CC* should be seen as collective opprobrium and outrage among groups of like-minded individuals (of diverse political persuasion) using social pressure to achieve cultural ostracism of targets accused of offensive/immoral words and deeds; it is thus a groupthink phenomenon driven by collective intentionality (Norris, 2023) and instantiated in recognizable and recurrent meso-level practices, *cancelation* (which are, as we will see below, clearly in flux). This distinction is key: *CC* is a Big C Conversation, as this macro-level analysis has shown. For its part, *cancelation* is a meso-level phenomenon that refers to the specific genre practices that carry out the sanctioning of norm-breaking individuals (Saint-Louis, 2021). Although the work on smart mobs and their connection to public shaming and indirectly to *CC* is interesting and relevant, it only describes part of the picture. More attention should be paid to how online *mobs* contingently come together with other on/offline groups to effectively carry out *cancelation*. Before we proceed on to the meso-level analysis, where this coming together is studied, the next section provides a necessary macro-level overview of the three case studies under examination.

4.3 Macro-Level Overview of the Three Case Studies

Cheney, DeGeneres, and Nichols were selected as their *cancelations*, although each unique, shared similar characteristics. The three *cancelees* are middle aged, white women, well known by the American public due to their jobs in media and politics. Their *cancelations* occurred within a similar timeframe and resulted in all of them facing serious consequences: both DeGeneres' and Nichols' shows (on NBC and ESPN, respectively) were canceled, and Cheney lost her executive position in the GOP as well as the primaries for her re-election as Wyoming House Representative. As a backdrop to the meso- and micro-level parts of the analysis, in the next section, I provide a detailed account of the triggers, consequences, and aftermath of the three *cancelations*.

4.3.1 Nichols

In August 2021. Nichols parted ways with ESPN (Entertainment and Sports Programming Network[12]) and her basketball program *The Jump* was canceled. This happened after the *New York Times*[13] reported, on July 4 of that same year, on derogatory comments Nichols had made regarding one of her colleagues, Maria Taylor (who is African American). In a 2020 conversation with a colleague from her room at the NBA's Walt Disney World bubble – unaware that her video camera was on, and she was being recorded to an ESPN server – Nichols said that Taylor had been selected to host the 2020 NBA finals instead of her because ESPN was feeling pressure on diversity.

This conversation, available to those ESPN employees with access to the server, was leaked to the *Times* a year later, although ESPN had long known about it, which set in motion hers and her show's *cancelation*. "I wish Maria Taylor all the success in the world – she covers football, she covers basketball," Nichols is heard saying on the tape. "If you need to give her more things to do because you are feeling pressure about your crappy longtime record on diversity – which, by the way, I know personally from the female side of it – like, go for it. Just find it somewhere else. You are not going to find it from me or taking my things away." Nichols later apologized on *The Jump*, saying she respected her ESPN colleagues and noting that she was "deeply, deeply sorry" for "disappointing those I hurt, particularly Maria Taylor."

---

[12] An affiliate of ABC, owned by the Walt Disney Co; the Hearst Corporation owns 20% of ESPN.
[13] www.nytimes.com/2021/07/04/sports/basketball/espn-rachel-nichols-maria-taylor.html.

4.3.2 DeGeneres

Nichols's *cancelation* trigger is quite straightforward, DeGeneres', however, is more multilayered, being attributed to various factors. Many point to Dakota Johnson's two awkward interviews with DeGeneres as the beginning of the end. In 2018, DeGeneres told Johnson she was offended because the latter had not invited her to her birthday party, even though DeGeneres had invited Johnson and her boyfriend (Chris Martin) to hers. When Johnson returned to the show in 2019, DeGeneres brought up not having been invited to Johnson's most recent birthday party, but Johnson promptly retorted that DeGeneres's statement was untrue, which was confirmed by one of the show's producers: DeGeneres had indeed been invited but had not attended. It soon came to light that, the day after the party, Louisiana-born DeGeneres – who is openly gay – had been seen cozying up to former President George W. Bush at a Dallas Cowboys' game; this caused a big uproar due to Bush's anti-LGBTQ policies and perceived failure to act during hurricane Katrina aftermath – which mostly affected the poor, amongst those many people of color – in DeGeneres home state.

Several other awkward interviews soon started to surface, which further pointed to a mismatch between DeGeneres's public "queen of nice" façade versus her "true" not so nice off-air personality. And then, in early 2020, comedian Kevin T. Porter tweeted a message mocking DeGeneres's purported kindness and inviting people to share their unkind stories with her, whom he described as one of the meanest people on earth, further undermining DeGeneres's public image. Porter pledged to match each story with $2 and to donate the full amount to a food bank. With over 2,600 replies at data collection point, Porter later said he had received about 300 stories detailing DeGeneres perceived meanness and ended up donating $600. Amid this climate, current and former employees of DeGeneres's show made public their complaints about the show's toxic atmosphere – for instance, a Black woman complained she had been the target of many "microaggressions" – and unfair treatment of employees during the COVID-19 pandemic.[14] Although related complaints were mostly directed at the show's producers, there was quite widespread consensus that DeGeneres was ultimately responsible for what happened on her show. She apologized both in a letter addressed to her staff and on air, to her audience, during the first show of the 18th season of her show. Despite her seemingly heartfelt apologies, after 19 seasons, the final episode of DeGeneres' daytime talk show aired on Thursday, May 26, 2022, on NBC.

---

[14] www.buzzfeednews.com/article/krystieyandoli/ellen-employees-allege-toxic-workplace-culture.

4.3.3 Cheney

Liz Cheney, a Republican, served as Representative for the state of Wyoming. Cheney's voting record shows her to have been one of the most stalwart conservative members of the House; in this, she closely followed in the footsteps of her own father, Dick B. Cheney, who served as President George W. Bush's Vice President for two consecutive terms (2001–2009) and is often viewed as the most powerful Vice President in American history. Congresswoman Cheney was not doing too badly herself. In 2016, she was chosen House Republican Conference Chair, which effectively made her the number 3 Republican in the chamber.

All this was to change, however. In the aftermath of the January 6, 2021 insurrection and during the second impeachment trial of former President Donald Trump, Cheney was one of ten Republican representatives who voted along with Democrats to impeach him. The dissidents would come to face dire consequences. Even before the impeachment formally ended, Wyoming Republicans overwhelmingly censured Cheney for her vote against Trump. A few months later, on May 12, 2021, in a voice vote behind closed doors, the House Republicans ousted Cheney from her leadership position. As he left the House, right after the vote, Congressman Ken Buck (Republican, Colorado) stated "Liz Cheney was canceled today for speaking her mind and disagreeing with the narrative that President Trump has put forth."[15]

Cheney's position within the GOP did not improve when she agreed to serve, as one of two minority members, on the Select Committee to investigate the January 6th attack on the US Capitol. Concerted efforts, ostensibly led by Trump, were put in place to derail her reelection bid, held in August 2022. Despite repeatedly denouncing the *Big Lie* (Trump's contention that he, not Biden, had won the presidential elections) and, thus, antagonizing her party's majority, Congresswoman Cheney was nonetheless hopeful that her strong conservative record would matter more than anything else for Wyoming voters (a state where Trump obtained 70% of the vote, a higher share than anywhere else in the country). Her hopes did not materialize, and – after a fierce campaign – Cheney lost to Trump-endorsed Harriet Hageman in the primaries. Hageman went on to secure Wyoming's only congressional seat.

Far from apologizing, Cheney has made her rebuke of Trumpism her brand and the platform on which she is rumored to perhaps run for President. Relatedly, in her concession speech, after losing the 2022 primaries, Cheney stated: "Two years ago, I won with 73% of the vote. I could easily have done so again. But it would have required that I go along with Trump's lies about the

---

[15] www.washingtonpost.com/opinions/2021/05/12/cancel-culture-republicans-just-canceled-liz-cheney/.

2020 election. That was a path I would not take. No House seat is more important than the principles we are all sworn to protect."[16]

5 Meso-Level Analysis: *Cancelation* as a Genre Ecology

This section is keyed to RQ2: What genre, meso-level, practices are involved in *cancelation*? Although research (Saint-Louis, 2021) has insightfully pointed to the conceptual differences between *CC* and *cancelation*, no discourse-based analysis to date has offered a detailed description of the meso-level practices deployed to carry out *cancelation*. However, *cancelation* is now a recognizable (in Garfinkel's sense) practice. This section aims to fill in this void.

A targeted meso-level analysis seeks to unveil the constituent social practices that make up *cancelation* and to relate them to the broader social structures and contexts that enable and shape said practices (such as, among others, social media platforms, workplaces, or legal systems). It also probes how practices can be used to challenge or transform these structures and institutions.

5.1 Methods

5.1.1 Data Sampling

The understanding of the genre practices involved in *cancelation*, used as background 31 cases of *cancelation* included in the reference *CC Corpus* (309,246 words and 256 videos) out of which three cases – described earlier, that is, Cheney, DeGeneres, and Nichols – were selected for detailed analysis.

All three cases and corresponding documentation were freely accessible in the public domain. Currently, public discourse refers to political or social debates found in newspapers, magazines, television, films, radio, music, and web-mediated forums (Marlow, 2017). Therefore, the research design based on related data did not need Institutional Review Approval.

5.1.2 Theoretical Framework and Procedure of Analysis

To present a nuanced description of *cancelation*, this level of the analysis applied the tenets of, among others, Rhetorical Genre Theory that views genre as social action (Miller, 1984; Bazerman, 1997, among others) and ESP (Swales, 1990) to the data. More specifically, I draw from Spinuzzi and Zachry's (2000) conceptualization of genre ecologies as an open-system framework to tackle the complexity of *cancelation* practices. A genre ecology includes an "interrelated group of genres (artifact types and the interpretive habits that have developed around them) used to jointly accomplish complex

---

[16] https://twitter.com/Liz_Cheney/status/1560966835943645184.

objectives" (172). Although prior research has shown that genres, as discussed, are not static but dynamic and fuzzy, the authors argue that to account for variation "a more robust ecological perspective is required, one that accounts for the dynamism and interconnectedness of genres" (173).

Genre ecologies are thus characterized by contingency, decentralization, and stability. By contingency, the authors refer to uncertainty in the sense that the relationship among genres in each ecology involves, "complex, opportunistic, sometimes risky coordination among genres that are made by people who are trying to accomplish certain things" (Spinuzzi & Zachry, 2000: 173). Decentralization, for its part, refers to usability, design, and intention being spread across the ecology of genres, not self-contained within individual genres. Finally, stability is seen as the tendency to make the interconnections among the different genres in the ecology conventional and official; therefore, "just as genres themselves are relatively stable while still being dynamic ... genre ecologies achieve relative stability – a dynamic equilibrium – over time. In relatively stable genre ecologies, certain connections among genres become commonplace: groups of users tend to use and interconnect genres in quite similar ways" (175). What is also interesting about the genre ecology conceptualization is that it is considered open-ended as users can import genres into the ecology in an ad hoc manner to help achieve its overarching goals (180).

Regarding procedure, the meso-level analysis involved the tracking, both on legacy and social media, of the specific individual's *cancelation* from its inception to its outcome and thus considering and carefully documenting all the genre practices (both on and offline) needed to achieve each *cancelation*.

5.2 Results and Discussion: Three *Cancelations*, Three Genre Ecologies

Figures 4, 5, and 6 provide a visual illustration of the application of the genre ecology model to the *cancelation* processes of Cheney, DeGeneres, and Nichols.

These three figures illustrate the complex genre ecologies that needed to be put in place to effect the three *cancelation*s under scrutiny. The illustrations only scratch the surface of the inherent complexity of *cancelation* and, thus, do not aim at being comprehensive, as in all three cases, the genre ecologies contain a multiplicity of genres and/or other genre ecologies within them.

Just as with genres in general, it is the communicative purpose (i.e., the goals of anyone involved in an act of communication on a given occasion, which is intended to be recognized by the other participants) that triggers the genre ecology and sets it in motion. As we have discussed, the goals of the

Pragmatics

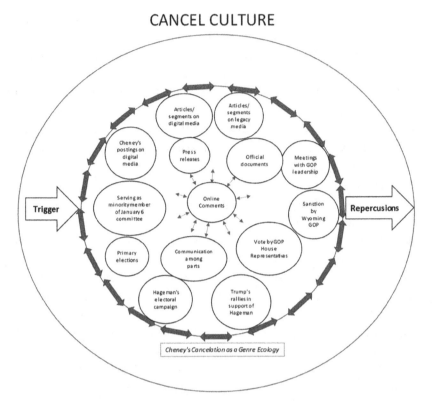

Figure 4 Cheney's cancelation as a genre ecology.

groups involved in *cancelation* are to expose and ostracize the *cancelee* and hold them accountable by making them face (financial, legal, etc.) consequences for their perceived transgressions. *Cancelation* also has a regulatory function as it is meant to dissuade others from potentially engaging in similar behavior or else.

Although the goals and ultimate consequences are similar, in the three cases here discussed, different interacting, interdependent systems of genres are needed to come together to achieve them. That is why the concept of genre ecology comes in handy, as it allows the addition of genres on ad hoc, contingent basis. Also, an ecology does not entail sequentiality (in the sense of one genre necessarily preceding another, as in a genre chain) but does show key interactivity (and potential simultaneity and iteration) among the genres (represented by arrows going in both directions in the illustration). Therefore, whereas it can be established that *cancelation* is now a recognizable practice, each instantiation will deploy some of the same genres along with specific ones, keyed to case-by-case requirements.

CANCEL CULTURE

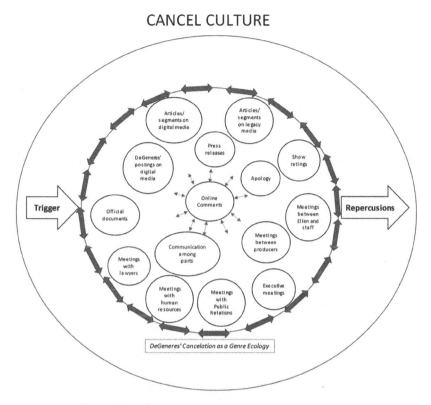

Figure 5 DeGeneres' cancelation as a genre ecology.

In the case of Nichols and DeGeneres, the goals of exposing, ostracizing, and holding them accountable for their perceived racism and lack of authenticity/ bad management skills that led to a toxic work environment triggered two similar genre ecologies that resulted in the *cancelation* of their shows and the termination of employment with ESPN and NBC, respectively. Cheney's *cancelation*, being ousted from her GOP leadership position and not re-elected as House representative, was by far the most complex (also at the micro-level, Section 6), and significantly distinct from the other two cases, in the sense of the genres involved, that is, many institutional and political genres not deployed elsewhere in the corpus.

It is interesting to note that all three *cancelations* contained a series of genre ecologies within the main genre ecology. For instance, the article on *The New York Times* detailing Nichol's transgression, which included the infamous audio of her conversation, is the result of a very complex genre ecology that involves other genre ecologies such as the leaking of information, the editorial process, and the publication process, all three – in turn – necessitating a multiplicity of

CANCEL CULTURE

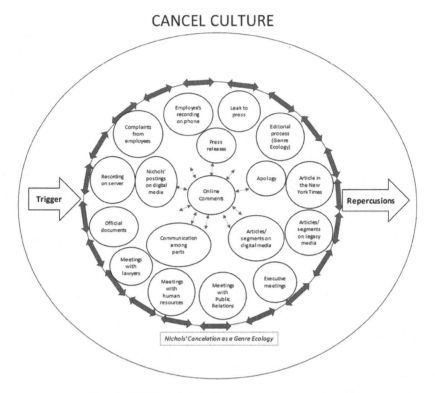

Figure 6 Nichols' cancelation as a genre ecology.

genres. The same can be said about the Buzzfeed piece that was the first to report on the toxicity on Ellen's show, albeit the publication process is here different as behooves an online-only outlet. This also applies, even to a much larger extent, to Cheney's case in which very intricate genre ecologies such as her opposer's electoral campaign and state primary elections, among others, which further require a wealth of genres/genre ecologies to come to fruition, were part of her *cancelation*.

In addition, the figures also show (as genres are collective, Miller, 1984) how all sorts of different groups – from thick to light, as discussed in Section 3) need to come together and act as an ad hoc agent to effect *cancelation*. Online "mobs," often related to *cancelation*, are just but a piece of this very complex groupal puzzle.

Crucially, all three-*cancelation* included what Swales (2004) has called *occluded* genres, genres that are out of sight, but perform essential backstage roles in *cancelation*. For Nichols and DeGeneres, occluded (ecologies of) genres were coordinated – among others – to facilitate meetings and discussions among network executives, between executives and Nichols and DeGeneres and their representatives, between executives and the public relations, human resources, and communications departments, between Nichols and DeGeneres and their lawyers, between the lawyers representing both parts, among others. For Cheney, behind closed-door voice votes, discussions among party leadership, between party leadership and Cheney, between Hageman and potential donors to and supporters of her electoral campaign, and so on, played a fundamental role in Cheney being ultimately canceled.

In addition, all three *cancelations* crucially consisted of a mix of online and offline genres (indeed it is currently very difficult to establish clear-cut differences between legacy – newspapers, television, radio, and so on – and digital media, as most legacy media are heavily represented online) that fed off and triggered each other as often, for instance, postings on social media by Nichols, DeGeneres, and Cheney in relation to their *cancelation* were reproduced and discussed on legacy media (TV shows segments, among others) and triggered, in turn, more postings and related commentary online. *CC* thus emerges as a prime example of the off/online nexus of post-digital societies (Blommaert, 2019), despite it having mostly been dealt with as an online phenomenon in the (non)academic literature (Section 4). Reaching similar conclusions, Norris (2023) argues that the role of digital media should be seen as reflecting and reinforcing *cancelation* practices by digital activists, rather than functioning as an independent driver of this phenomenon.

It is noteworthy that in all three cases, the *ultimate cancelation* was carried out by those holding executive power over the *cancelee*s, ESPN, NBC, the GOP, and Wyoming voters. However, that does not mean that *cancelation* is exclusively in the hands of powerful groups, as claimed by Saint-Louis (2021): it is unlikely that some of these *cancelations* would have occurred without the deployment of other genre practices and the continued and renewed reverberation and quick circulation of communicative resources such as via commentary, hashtags, and memes on dedicated online spaces. As the model predicts, the three genre ecologies are decentralized, with the ultimate purpose being spread across the ecology of genres, not self-contained within individual genres.

Results show that the online comments genre emerges as common and crucial to *cancelation* processes as commentary responds to the actions carried out by other genre practices in the ecology (as mentioned, for instance, in relation to comments in response to television segments recontextualized to social media) and thus reproduces and amplifies the process. Their centrality could be interpreted as a sine qua non condition for *cancelation* (as represented by the central position of online comments in Figures 4–6, and the arrows going in both directions pointing to the synergy between online comments and other genres in the ecology) and it is one of the reasons why online comments have been selected as the focus of this Element's micro-level analysis. In addition to its centrality, as discussed, many other genres in the ecologies are occluded which prevents the analyst's access and many of those that are not (newspaper articles, political rallies, television shows, campaign ads, public apologies, etc.) have already received significant attention in the pragmatics/discourse analysis/ sociolinguistics literature. Crucially, online comments were selected as a response to the call for micro-level analyses of *cancelation* which are to date very scarce and because they provide a window into light groups and collective intentionality and agency, as deliberation theorists see discussion as key in decision-making (Dryzek, 2007). Crucially online commentary is key to online public shaming, one of the main tools of *CC* and which will be explored, at the micro-level, in the next section.

6 Micro-Level Analysis

This part of the analysis addresses RQ3 that probes how *cancelation* is realized at the micro-level (with a focus on online practices) and how the micro-level resources used contribute to the light groups involved in *cancelation* becoming agents.

6.1 Methods

6.1.1 Data Sampling and Selection

An analytic corpus comprising circa 80,000 words, 2,220 comments was obtained from the reference *CC* corpus for this part of the analysis. These data were extracted from online interactions triggered by articles, social media videos, and posts related to the three cases described (roughly 740 comments per case). The first 300 comments posted (150 from the original publication and 150 from its reposting to Facebook in those cases where this applies; Table 1), responses, and metadata were manually downloaded with the "sort by" settings set to the "All comments" option. The analytic corpus was then cleaned, and comments were anonymized and numbered. Some were discarded for being off-topic or posted more than once. That brought the number to the circa 740 comments per *cancelation* case mentioned.

The main criteria for data selection, inspired by polymedia (Androutsopoulos, 2021) involved visibility and balancing of different ideological positions on the issue at hand. Therefore, Facebook pages were given preference. At the time of writing, Facebook is the top social media platform (2.99 billion monthly active users, followed by YouTube with 2.2 billion) and has the most spread out generational and gender demographics of all social media. For instance,

Table 1 Sources selected for micro-level analysis.

Cancelee	Sources: Comments triggered by	Relevant information
Liz Cheney	January 18, 2021 https://m.washingtontimes.com/news/2021/jan/18/liz-cheney-censured-wyoming-vote-impeach-donald-tr/?fbclid=IwAR18hSOC2FIKtTJVyGxc0ob1OcfONYwzWtSxcPpt7ikUr4ElnIUrw61zFHk www.facebook.com/ForAmerica/	Article in *The Washington Times* (a conservative outlet) posted to *ForAmerica*, a conservative advocacy group, Facebook page. In the article, Cheney's being censored by Wyoming Republicans is discussed.
	May 6, 2021 www.washingtonpost.com/opinions/2021/05/05/liz-cheney-republican-party-turning-point/?fbclid=IwAR3aQaKzrmgxDB9wMPMqzojfpdeepUIn2vB66xJah-yMF89cl2xeADOiWTE www.facebook.com/CheneyLiz	An op-ed signed by Liz Cheney and published in *The Washington Post* (a liberal-leaning outlet) in which she discusses the GOP and how they will be held accountable by future generations. Cheney posted the link to this op-ed to her Facebook page.
	May 12, 2021 www.washingtonpost.com/opinions/2021/05/12/cancel-culture-republicans-just-canceled-liz-cheney/	Op-ed by renowned political journalist Dana Milbank posted to *The Washington Post*'s webpage. In it, he discusses the Republican Party presenting itself as anti-*CC*, but also guilty of engaging in *cancelation* practices (Liz Cheney's).
Ellen DeGeneres	July 16, 2020 www.buzzfeednews.com/article/krystieyandoli/ellen-employees-allege-toxic-workplace-culture	Posted to the BuzzFeed news' webpage, this article was the first to denounce the alleged toxic atmosphere on DeGeneres' talk show after interviewing several (former) employees.
	August 25, 2020 www.youtube.com/watch?v=O2Oj9X2R35o	A video that comments on DeGeneres' *cancelation* posted to the YouTube's commentary channel *The Showest* that primarily discusses *movie/TV actors and other celebrities*.

Table 1 (cont.)

Cancelee	Sources: Comments triggered by	Relevant information
	May 13, 2021 www.nytimes.com/2021/05/13/opinion/culture/Ellen-Degeneres-show-canceled-relatability.html	Guest essay by Amil Niazi published *on The New York Times*' digital edition in which the reasons of DeGeneres' fall from grace are analyzed.
Rachel Nichols	August 25, 2021 www.cnn.com/2021/08/25/media/rachel-nichols-espn-the-jump/index.html www.facebook.com/cnn	Article reporting on Rachel Nichols' downfall, initially posted to CNN's webpage and reposted to CNN's Facebook's page the following day. CNN has traditionally been categorized as left of center/left but it has recently been claimed that the network's new corporate ownership is pulling it to the political right.
	August 25, 2021 www.facebook.com/RachelNicholsTV	Rachel Nichols' post on her *Facebook* page thanking *The Jump*'s fans and hinting at new professional ventures after leaving ESPN.
	August 26, 2021 www.foxnews.com/media/espn-maria-taylor-rachel-nichols	Article posted to Fox News' (a conservative outlet) webpage criticizing ESPN's handling of Nichols' case.

Twitter has only 436 million monthly active users many of those being in the 25–34-year bracket (38.5%) and mostly male[17] (56.4%). When the original posts were shared by news and advocacy organizations, those that represented the breadth of the political ideological spectrum as well as more personal sources such as the *cancelee*s' profile pages were selected (Table 1).

Regarding ethical considerations, all sources included in the corpus had their privacy settings set to *public,* which means information posted to them is visible to anyone who accesses the page and is thus in the public domain. Therefore, the data and research design were exempt from Institutional Review Board approval. Nonetheless, and in compliance with the Association of Internet Researchers' ethical recommendations for best practices,[18] all potential personal identifiers were removed. For the most part, comments will be discussed in aggregate form – that is, results will be compiled and summarized – and those that are used as illustrations may also be slightly rephrased to further avoid personal identification. In the discussion, comments will appear in their original form, including any spelling, grammar, and punctuation idiosyncrasies.

6.1.1.1 Data: The Genre of Online Comments

Online comments were selected to be the focus of this segment of the analysis. Online comments constitute public discourse, which reflects and reinforces intergroup relations, the focus of this Element. Although traditionally mediated public discourse has been in the hands of the powerful (van Dijk, 1995), online public discourse (with caveats) is more egalitarian and helps fuel Big C Conversations, such as *CC* (Romano, 2020).

More specifically, online comments are a common genre of digital communication and are often central to the affordances of most social media platforms. Indeed, user-generated comments are at the heart of participatory culture, the commodification of language and linguistic capitalism (Thornton, 2018), are the main target of dataveillance, and constitute some of the major bases upon which our algorithmic identities are constructed (Cheney-Lippold, 2017). The pervasiveness of online comments has made social networks complex, multi-authored, multicultural, multimodal virtual spaces (Benson, 2017) that offer prime loci for the triggering of feelings of groupness and collective identity, and crucially for this

---

[17] https://buffer.com/library/social-media-sites/.
https://bloggingwizard.com/twitter-statistics/.
www.statista.com/statistics/187549/facebook-distribution-of-users-age-group-usa/#:~:
text=U.S.%20Facebook%20users%202022%2C%20by%20age%20group&text=As%20of%
20December%202022%2C%2023.7,largest%20audience%20in%20the%20country.
Please note that numbers can fluctuate.   [18] https://aoir.org/ethics/.

Element, rich sites for civic engagement, and grassroots activism (Androutsopoulos & Tereick, 2015).

Regarding their main communicative purpose, online comments are (short, albeit length substantially varies and may be sometimes constrained) responses to an original post or to other responses to said post. It is not infrequent, however, to find unrelated comments when analyzing threads. Responses tend to be extremely varied in content – they can contain the whole gamut of speech acts, indeed multiple speech acts are often contained within a response – and can, thus, serve different functions. In that sense, online comments can be compared, with some caveats, to a turn at talk in a sequence, or a thread here (Frobenius & Gerhardt, 2017). Some of these caveats are related to the fact that online interactions are polylogal (Bou-Franch & Garcés-Conejos Blitvich 2014; Garcés-Conejos Blitvich, 2010a) rather than dyadic, which fundamentally alters their nature by making them even more multifunctional and heightening levels of performativity (as one plays, as it were, to multiple audiences). Other caveats concern, as mentioned, online comments responding to more than one addressee or group of addresses, via tags and @mentions for instance, and often being multimodal and including semiotic modes other than language.

Regarding rhetorical strategies, the register of online comments is generally casual, informal texts exchanged between equals, which are personal and abbreviated and tend to rely on experiences and values not to adhere to standard grammar conventions and be highly multimodal and often hyperbolic. They fall into what Thorne and Reinhardt (2008: 562) refer to as "vernacular digital language conventions" and can often be aggressive and use impolite and profane language (Chen, 2020; Lorenzo-Dus et al., 2011). However, due to the inherent diversity of online groups, other registers such as formal – that is, that associated with workplace and academic contexts, and so on, and thus displaying evidence for claims, citing sources, being critically oriented, and following the conventions of Standard English – can be also found (Garcés-Conejos Blitvich & Lorenzo-Dus, 2022). Further, depending on the platform, intimate registers, that is, texts between family and loved ones (Joos, 1967) are also a staple.

6.1.2 Theoretical Framework and Procedure of Analysis

The general approach to the data is netnographic – and thus qualitative and non-media centric – and aims to offer a thick description (Geertz, 1973) of the online *cancelation* practices of light groupings. More specifically, it constitutes a descriptive netnography (Addeo et al., 2019) which means the analysis is theoretically driven with the aim of filling a gap in the literature and providing detailed information about a less researched phenomenon. My role within the light group was that of a lurker,[19] as participants were not aware of my presence or research aims. This *covert* form of netnography allows not only for an unintrusive, invisible exploration and collection of natural data during which members do not modify their behavior in ways related to the observer's paradox but also for the unpredictability of results associated with this type of analysis.

In consonance with the tenets of netnography, the analytic corpus underwent a thematic analysis with the help of NVivo 1.6.1, designed for qualitative researchers working with very rich text-based and/or multimedia information, where deep levels of analysis are required. Further, thematic analysis (Fereday & Muir-Cochrane, 2006) offers an accessible and theoretically flexible approach to analyzing data. It involves recording or identifying passages of text or images that are linked by a common theme or idea. Themes are patterns across data sets that are important to the description of a phenomenon and are associated with (a) specific research question(s). In addition, and importantly for this study as described below, NVivo's matrix coding query option facilitates relevant data linking, which provides further insights into networks of information.

The coding of the corpus was carried out by the author and her research assistant and took a *second-order approach* (Watts, 2003), in the sense that it reflects the analysts' views regarding the phenomena scrutinized. Nonetheless, and due to its ethnographic and discursive ethos, the analysis also strove to reflect participants' own assessments of the interactions. The multilayered nature of the analysis, from a theoretical standpoint, and the fact that each *cancelation*, although similar in many respects, required the development of case-specific codes led to lengthy discussions (over ten hours) during which we first familiarized ourselves with the data, assigned and labeled preliminary, parent codes, which were selected based on having the most analytic value and were sometimes later modified, applying a hermeneutic circle, as we developed a deeper understanding of the data set. A hierarchal structure was then created by adding clusters of child codes under each parent code as patterns/themes in the corpus emerged; this process continued until coding saturation was achieved. Although parent codes remained quite stable during the coding process, some were eliminated at a later stage due to lesser relevance. Often, more than one recurrent theme came up in a comment, in which case said comment was coded for different themes. However, each comment was coded just *once for each theme*, even if the theme appeared multiple times within the same comment. For instance, every comment was coded for different types of

---

[19] See Addeo et al. (2019) for a discussion of the pros and cons of overt and covert ethnography.

(im)politeness present; however, each type was only coded once, even if there were more cases of the same (im)politeness type present. Detailed notes about our field observations were taken and shared via NVivo's *annotations*, and weekly meetings were held to compare the coding results and to resolve any intercoder differences. Intercoder reliability remained high (above 96.5%) during the entire process.

Regarding the creation of the coding scheme, and to address the third research question, the analysis drew from a range of interdisciplinary sources. Notions of identity construction, claims, attributions, and (non) verification were central and applied following the frameworks and conceptualizations proposed by Bucholtz and Hall (2005) and Joseph (2013). Since *cancelation* had been critically related to morality (Section 4.2), the influential work by social psychologist Jonathan Haidt (and colleagues) underlaid the interpretation of the identity co-construction process. Crucial to this understanding was Moral Foundations Theory (Haidt, 2012). Drawing from evolutionary psychology to explain their origin, the theory proposes that several innate and universally available psychological systems are the foundations of "intuitive ethics." These five foundations are summarized in Figure 7.

In addition, Haidt et al.[20] believe that there are several other good candidates for "*foundationhood*," such as:

	Adaptive Challenge	Original Triggers	Current Triggers	Characteristic Emotions	Relevant Virtues
Care / Harm	Protect and care for children	Suffering, distress, or neediness expressed by onus's child	Baby seals, cute cartoon characters	Compassion	Caring, kindness
Fairness / Cheating	Reap benefits of two-way partnership	Cheating, cooperation, deception	Marital fidelity, broken vending machines	Anger, gratitude, guilt	Fairness, justice, trustworthiness
Loyalty / Subversion	Form, cohesive, coalitions	Threat or challenge to group	Sports teams, nations	Group pride, rage at traitors	Loyalty, patriotism, self-sacrifice
Sanctity / Degradation	Avoid contamination	Waste products, diseased people	Taboo ideas (communism, racism)	Disgust	Temperance, chastity, piety, cleanliness

Figure 7 Moral foundations,

---

[20] https://moralfoundations.org/.

Liberty/oppression: the feelings of reactance and resentment people feel toward those who dominate them and restrict their freedom. Its intuitions are often in tension with those of the authority foundation. For instance, hatred of bullies and dominators may motivate people to come together, in solidarity, to oppose or take down the oppressor.

Also due to the very close connections established between *CC* and emotions (Section 4.2), the analysis explored the data to identify patterns of moral emotions expressed when reacting to and evaluating the *cancelee*'s or the *ultimate canceler*'s behavior. According to Haidt (2003: 853), moral emotions are those "that are linked to the interests or welfare either of society as a whole or at least of persons other than the judge or agent." Applying Haidt's classification, both parent and child codes were created for these moral emotions "families" (Figure 8):

In the case of suffering emotions and following Haidt (2003) who argued that empathy is not a moral emotion and, for their part, compassion and sympathy are hard to tease apart, all suffering emotions were merged into a single category: compassion/sympathy.

CC is often portrayed as highly uncivil. As discussed, online incivility includes – among others – many different forms of language aggression. Within pragmatics, language aggression has mostly been studied from the point of view of impoliteness models, where impoliteness is generally understood as behavior that causes offense. Impoliteness is always situated, that is, it is an attitude toward specific behaviors occurring in specific contexts when there is a mismatch between these behaviors and how one would expect/want/

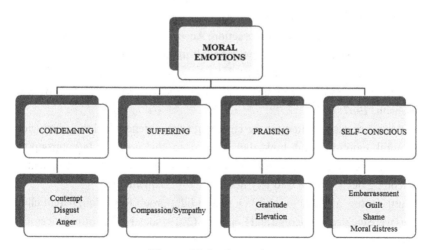

Figure 8 Moral emotions

think they ought to be (Culpeper, 2011: 254). The analysis of aggression was based on Culpeper's (2016: 441) classification of impoliteness, and child codes were created accordingly. Additionally, in a bottom-up fashion, the following impoliteness manifestation not included in the extant taxonomy emerged in the analysis and were added as child codes to the codebook:

> Disagreements: these are not inherently impolite (Angouri & Locher, 2012); however, in this oppositional discourse, they were essential to the processes of in/out group identity construction (claims, attributions, and non/verification).

Importantly, impoliteness is functional and can be used to achieve aims such as forcing (attempting to force) others to succumb to one's will, what Culpeper (2011: 226) describes as *coercive* impoliteness; impoliteness can also be used as the targeted display of heightened emotion, mostly anger, implying that the target is to blame for producing such emotional state, that is, *affective* impoliteness (Culpeper, 2011: 252). These two functions of impoliteness are salient in the corpus, as results show.

In addition, using the classification of strategies provided by Brown and Levinson (1987), politeness manifestations were also analyzed. My point of departure, as mentioned, is aligned with views of (im)politeness as situated (Davies et al., 2011). That clearly diverges from Brown and Levinson's initial understanding of some speech acts as *intrinsically* face-threatening. Situated impoliteness means that it is speakers in certain contexts, not linguistic expressions per se, that are assessed as (im)polite. Relatedly, although there has been some discussion regarding the need to do away with the distinction between negative and positive face (Bousfield, 2008), I agree with Culpeper (2016) and have long argued (Garcés-Conejos Blitvich, 2010b) that this distinction (with caveats) remains theoretically useful and reflects central behaviors observed in human interaction. Accordingly, negative face is understood as "the want of very 'competent adult member' that his [sic] actions be unimpeded by others" whereas positive face is seen as "the want of every member that his [sic] wants be desirable to at least some others" (Brown & Levinson, 1987: 61).

Codes were also created for the targets of (im)politeness and the expression of moral emotions and how they related to the poster's in/outgroup(s). Positionings regarding the out/ingroup are highly situated, and vary frequently, and coding decisions need to rely necessarily on sequentiality.

Furthermore, and due to their key role in light group formation, parent/child codes were created for George and Leidner's (2019) social media affordances and activism classification (Digital *Spectator* activities [including Metavoicing, Clicktivism/Assertion], *Transitional* activities [including Political consumerism;

Digital petitions; Botivism; E-funding] and *Gladiatorial* activities [including Data activism; Exposure; Hacktivism]). Finally, notions of geo-semiotics (Scollon & Wong Scollon, 2003) and emotional geographies (Davidson et al., 2005) were also applied for a deeper understanding of the data.

Once the coding was completed, and with the help of NVivo, several main matrix coding queries were run. These included select parent and child codes and aimed to examine relevant coding intersections. The results of these queries helped unveil further patterns in the data and provided access to the content in which those patterns occurred, which added nuance to the results and informed the discussion.

6.2 Results and Discussion of the Micro-Level Analysis: Online *Cancelation* Practices

As framing to the rest of the analysis, let's first discuss the results of the coding regarding George and Leidner's (2019) classification and digital media affordances in general. As pointed out by Saint-Louis (2021), several activities placed at different levels of engagement with activism are part and parcel of *cancelation*. In the corpus, just *digital spectator* activities Clicktivism (liking) and Metavoicing (Sharing, reporting, and commenting) were present: another reason behind the analytic focus on comments. Further, comments were eminently textual (emojis occurred 93 times; gifs 7; hashtags 3; hyperlinks 14; no memes were present). Therefore, language was the mode of choice for *cancelers* and, thus, analysts.

6.2.1 Identity Claims/Attributions/(Non)verification: Morality and Degradation Ceremonies

Concerning *CC* generally, the micro-level analysis revealed a more complex picture of *cancelation* than previously described in the literature, which just refers to two waves of *CC* led by liberal and conservative groups, respectively. The data showed the simultaneous enacting of both waves, but not necessarily attached to political persuasion, and it further uncovered combinations of *cancelation* targets.

Three distinct *cancelation* processes emerged:

1. Straightforward *cancelation* of *cancelee* (Cheney, DeGeneres, Nichols)
2. Showing dissent with *cancelation*/supporting the *cancelee*: the *ultimate canceler* (the GOP, NBC/the general public, ESPN) is subject to *cancelation* (by not watching its shows, discontinuing membership to channels, not voting its candidates/actively supporting opponents, etc.)
3. Both the *cancelee and* the ultimate *canceler* are subject to *cancelation*

Cheney's and Nichols' cases involved, to varying degrees, the three *cancelation* types described above. In DeGeneres', just the first two were identified. Having been numbered 1–3 does not indicate sequentiality (as they are simultaneous) but the order in which they have been accounted for.

What these three *cancelation* types share are the centrality of identity construction processes, regarding both self-positioning and attribution (Jones, 2017). Engaging in *cancelation* implies assuming the identity *canceler* and, thereby, displaying the attributes and collective intentionality associated with the ecology, that is, to expose/denounce *cancelees* and/or the ultimate *cancelers*, make them accountable, and deter third parties. Identities are relational (Bucholtz & Hall, 2005: 598), so *alterity*, or otherness, is key here (as subject positions are constructed by qualifying others).

Importantly, in relation to the different *cancelation* types that emerged, results showed that in 762 occurrences *cancelees* (Cheney, DeGeneres, and Nichols) were attributed a negative social identity. However, in 783 different occurrences, other *cancelers* showed dissent by associating *cancelees* instead with positive aspects *but* attributing a negative social identity to the *ultimate cancelers* (GOP, NBC/General Public, ESPN). By doing so, the first groups of *cancelers* relationally constructed opposing subject positions (Au, 2017) for themselves: that is, nonracist, authentic, constitutionalist, pro-free speech. Other *cancelers*, for their part, by not ratifying the negative identity attributions and showing dissent, ascribed positive characteristics either to the *cancelee* and/ or the ultimate *canceler,* thus, justifying not engaging in their specific *cancelation*. This shows that – far from being homogeneous – *cancelation* processes are fractured and involve a multiplicity of out/ingroups, as illustrated below. In all cases, the negative identities attributed, as predicted by prior research, were strongly related to perceived moral failings (Mueller, 2021; Norris, 2023).

Regarding Nichols, see Table 2, she and her ingroup undergo *cancelation* mostly for being considered racist, as shown in Example 1. Racism is here related to the not upholding of the Harm/Care foundation (Haidt, 2012) regarding the ability to feel the pain of others, especially more vulnerable populations.

Table 2 Nichols' *cancelation.*

Target of cancelation	1st *cancelation* type	2nd *cancelation* type	3rd *cancelation* type
Nichols/ingroup	Cancel	Support	Cancel
ESPN	Support	Cancel	Cancel

Example 1
I am OUTRAGED! Rachel Nichols is a vile racist, homophobe, misogynist, ageist, fat shamer who DESERVED EXACTLY WHAT SHE GOT!!!!

On a second process, she is constructed as having positive characteristics: non-racist, truthful, etc., see Example 2:

Example 2
I support Rachel in all of this. Her comments were nothing more than truth.

It is her former employer and *ultimate canceler* (ESPN) that undergoes *cancelation* for *wokeness*, i.e., caving to liberal pressures, as illustrated in Example 3.

Example 3
The canceling of Nichols is a window on an America controlled by the now far-left Democrats. In such a world, one must not deviate at all from the accepted norms of the leftist mob. Violators are canceled and publicly shamed – in order to discourage others from not conform leftist behavioral standards . . . ESPN has become an authoritarian entity.

ESPN is thus assessed as not upholding the Fairness/Cheating and the Loyalty/Betrayal foundations, for firing Nichols unfairly and not showing loyalty to an outstanding employee.

The third *cancelation*-type positions *both* Nichols and ESPN as deserving of *cancelation*. Nichols for being *woke*, *liberal*, a *hypocrite*. ESPN, in turn, for terminating someone's employment who just expressed an opinion, wrongly perceived as racist, thus also displaying *wokeness,* as pointed out in Example 4. Here, we observe a reaction – related to the Liberty/Oppression foundation – to caving to *liberal* and *woke* forces that restrict liberty of expression and action:

Example 4
What Rachel said wasn't wrong, but it was hypocritical. Live by the "woke," die by the "woke."

Occurrences related to *cancelation* processes 2 and 3 were mostly found in the Fox News Webpage comments, a conservative outlet, and are thus closely aligned with accounts of the second wave of *CC*.

Cheney's *cancelation* also shows complexity and can be ascribed to political persuasion more clearly than Nichols' and certainly Degeneres' (Table 3). A first type – related to the first wave of *CC* albeit not led by liberals, as claimed (Section 4.2) – we find Republicans who attribute to Cheney and her ingroup *RINO* (Republican in name only), *traitor*, and *disloyal* social

Table 3 Cheney's *cancelation.*

Target of cancelation	1st *cancelation* type	2nd *cancelation* type	3rd *cancelation* type
Cheney/ingroup	Cancel	Support	Cancel
Trumpist GOP	Support	Cancel	Cancel

identities (see Example 5); this group wholeheartedly supports Cheney's ousting from her leadership position and encourages Wyoming voters not to reelect her (Example 6). Cheney and her ingroup are perceived as having undermined the Loyalty/Betrayal foundation by not supporting Trump, the GOP's leader, and the Authority/Subversion by not respecting the wishes of those who elected and put her in a leadership position:

Example 5
Liz, your sudden Constitutionalist conversion is unconvincing. It's also worth noting that the majority of your support is coming from Marxist ideologues.
You know what they say, "if she walks a RiNO and talks a RiNO . . . ."
GAME OVER Liz.

Example 6
I hope the good people of Wyoming primary this spineless hack and replace her with a true constitutionalist.

The second type here involves both conservatives, independents, *and* liberals. Conservatives consider themselves, and Cheney, to be constitutionalists and flatly reject Trumpism: it is the Trumpist GOP who should pay dearly for not voting in favor of Trump's second impeachment and mistreating such a staunch conservative, as argued in Example 7,

Example 7
you don't want us to post facts about what a conservative Republican definition is, do you??? Because dear, Ms. Cheney is one of THE most conservative Republicans around. YOUR Republican Party doesn't represent anything of the Lincoln or even Reagan party. It is YOU who has messed up principles and values.

Many democrats/independents in this group, who share no ideological common ground with her, admire Cheney's courage and agree it is the GOP that is at fault and should be penalized accordingly (see Example 8 and Example 9).

Example 8

Sending you Respect, **Liz Cheney**, from a Brooklyn born Upstate New York lifelong Democrat, age 75. Your courage is admirable and inspirational.

Example 9

. . . I am not even a republican. I'm an independent. I'd vote for a Cheney Romney ticket, maybe even over the dem party.

All in all, the Trumpist GOP is seen as not sustaining the Loyalty/Betrayal foundation, and having rejected patriotism by putting party, instead of country, first.

The third *cancelation*-type involves democrats and independents who profoundly dislike/disagree with Cheney's very conservative voting record – perceived as not upholding the Harm/Care foundation, since many policies she has supported may have hurt women and other minorities – and liken her to her father, Vice-President Cheney. This group thinks, as argued in Example 10, that her recent anti-Trump stance is not enough to redeem Cheney, while also deploring and exposing the actions of the Trumpist GOP, which is assessed (also Example 7) as not maintaining the Loyalty/Betrayal foundation by not abiding by the USA's constitution:

Example 10

Hey, she's her Daddy's daughter . . . that apple didn't even fall off the tree. She and her Daddy are part and parcel as to why the GOP is where they are today. Maybe she is telling the truth, but she doesn't get a "Get Out of Jail Free" card at this point in time. She could have said plenty before the insurrection . . . and she didn't. And, in fact, she voted lock, stock, and barrel with Donnie every single time. Maybe she didn't say she was "racist" out loud, but it's there. I remember the vile crap her dad did to this country and I don't trust her as far as I can throw her. In addition to her throwing her sister under the bus because she is gay.

For DeGeneres (Table 4), a first *cancelation*-type involves exposing her as *fake* or *inauthentic* – that is, putting up a sham *nice* facade to maintain her popularity, but truly being *mean, cruel, fake, sadistic* – and (at least) partially responsible for the toxic climate on her show, as argued in Example 11:

Example 11

I think what people are "happy" about is the fact that Ellen put out this image of sweetness and kindness as well as this "holier than thou" attitude and she it turns out it was just an act, she was also judgemental towards

Table 4 Ellen's *cancelation* (no third type present).

Target of *cancelation*	1st *cancelation* type	2nd *cancelation* type
Ellen/ingroup	Cancel	Support
NBCPublic/*CC*	Support	Cancel

people who weren't as kind as she was, but it turns out she's not nearly as kind or sweet as she claims to be. It seems they're happy to feel validated because they knew the truth.

This view surmises DeGeneres' behavior as not upholding either the Fairness/Cheating foundation, by pretending to be different from whom she really is in order to be liked, and the Loyalty/Betrayal for betraying the audience's confidence. Further, by her alleged mistreatment of employees, DeGeneres is perceived as not supporting the Care/Harm foundation.

In a second *cancelation*-type, more difficult to relate to a distinct political ideology (although DeGeneres is openly gay and liberal), she is constructed as either *genuine or not genuine* (but posters argue that one should separate the *person* from the *host*) and, importantly, as a *victim of societal misogyny*, as discussed in Example 12).

Example 12
I think Ellen herself is to blame for very little of it. Cancel culture tends to be rather sexist, and society is quick to "cancel" successful women in positions of power. I think Ellen should be held accountable for some of these things, but the higher ups behind the scenes whose names we maybe don't know also need to hold themselves accountable and enact change.

Further, as illustrated by Example 13, Ellen is portrayed as human and, as such, prone to making mistakes. Her apologizing publicly and privately (to her employees) garnered her further support, as some may see obtaining an apology as the goal of *CC* (Mueller, 2021).

Example 13
Ellen is human. She gets agitated, anxious and sometimes angry like the rest of us . . . And she did apologize for times she came up short, or could've done better.

Here, those who are exposed are *CC* and the public for believing unsub-stantiated information and showering hate on her and NBC for ultimately *canceling* DeGeneres' talk show. The former is seen as not sustaining the

Harm/Care foundation for destroying DeGeneres' career based on unproven allegations or by setting irrational standards for her. *The ultimate canceler*, NBC, is negatively assessed for caving to the authority of the mob and not supporting such an outstanding, highly recognized show (which had won, among others, 34 Daytime Emmy Awards) and, therefore, not upholding the Liberty/Oppression foundation and the Loyalty/Betrayal foundation, respectively.

As shown, in the three *cancelation* types, the *cancelee/ultimate canceler* and the group they are associated with are subject to radical identity reduction, oversimplification, and stigmatization (Goffman, 1963a), that is, they are defined by a single, negatively valenced attribute: *fake, racist, RINO, unconstitutionalist, woke*, and so on. This is reminiscent of a *degradation ceremony*, that is, the communicative work that transforms a person's entire status and identity into something lower (Garfinkel, 1956). This ceremony is, essentially, quite an aggressive, and necessarily collective, process whereby an individual/group identity is debased and is tied to moral outrage/indignation and public denunciation (21). *Cancelers* feel justified in publicly shaming, socially excluding, and ostracizing *cancelees/ultimate cancelers*, because the latter and their ingroup were reduced to mere immoral beings/entities. In this respect, it has been argued that "[o]nline settings reduce empathic distress by representing other people as two-dimensional icons whose suffering is not readily visible" (Crockett, 2017: 770). This is where, as we will discuss below, the dark side of morality emerges (Monroe & Ashby Plant, 2019). Here, as well, we see in action the three processes described by Tajfel and Turner (1979/2004) involved in the qualifying of others: social categorization, social identification, and social comparison. The authors argued regarding the third that, in being compared, one's ingroup needed to come out as being better or having some sort of higher status than the outgroup. In the processes under scrutiny, groups compete for higher moral ground and most respected objective morality.

Identity claims/attributions/reduction, (non)verification, and concomitant processes of othering versus affiliation are key to the process of gelling online light groups and the first step toward achieving group agency during digital degradation ceremonies. Results show, and this is an important finding, that online spaces reflect and co-construct offline ideologies, as there is more than one group and more than one ideology at work although both share a similar collective intentionality, *cancelation* albeit of different targets. Results also show that conservatives can lead *cancelation* and that *cancelation* is a more complex process than initially described and that there is more than one "mob" involved in *cancelation* processes.

6.2.2 (Im)politeness Manifestations

As seen, the processes of social identity claims/ attributions and (non)verification play an essential role in in/outgroup formation. We need to further probe how these very light online out/in groups quickly gel and gain enough entitativity and agency to join or encourage other light/thick groups related to the vast array of contingent genres involved in each *cancelation* ecology to accomplish its collective intentionality. These key queries were also answered through a detailed micro-analysis of the digital data.

To that end, and due to the key role that (im)politeness plays in ratifying, modulating, and modifying the social relationships associated with certain social identities (Jones, 2017), the next part of the analysis focused on (im) politeness manifestations in the corpus. Importantly, *CC* and related practices, such as online public shaming, are inevitably portrayed as a punitive and aggressive phenomenon that seeks to disqualify *cancelees* and associated groups for perceived moral failings (Goldman, 2015). Further, as described, the corpus is made up of online comments a genre that follows what Thorne and Reinhardt (2008: 562) labeled as "vernacular digital language conventions" and can be often aggressive and use impolite and profane language (Chen, 2020); therefore, the presence of impoliteness in the corpus was anticipated. This proved to be the case as the coding process unveiled 4,288 occurrences – 51.7% of impoliteness. Not as anticipated, however, was the almost equally significant presence of politeness with 3,999 occurrences – 48.3% (total occurrences 8,287 – 100%).

To further probe these unexpected results, a coding matrix query was run to check for meaningful intersections between two sets of parent codes [(im) politeness and out/ingroup]. As shown in Tables 5 and 6, a clear pattern emerged: impoliteness was mostly directed intergroup whereas politeness was directed intragroup. In this case, each *comment* was coded only *once* for either intergroup (im)politeness or intragroup (im)politeness (totaling 3,112

Table 5 (Im)politeness in comments and the in/outgroups.

Target of impoliteness	# Comments in corpus	Percentage of total (rounded)
Intergroup politeness	313	10
Intergroup impoliteness	1,234	40
Intragroup politeness	1,264	40
Intragroup impoliteness	301	10
Total	3,112	100

Table 6 (Im)politeness per case and file.

	Intergroup impoliteness	Percentage of total	Intergroup politeness	Percentage of total	Intragroup impoliteness	Percentage of total	Intragroup politeness	Percentage of total	Totals	Percentage of total
Cheney:										
For America on FB	92		32		111		142		377	
Liz Cheney FB Page	95		58		50		106		309	
The Washington Times	122		62		25		118		327	
The Washington Post	147		84		39		149		419	
Total	456	15%	236	8%	225	7%	515	17%	1,432	46%
DeGeneres:										
Buzzfeed News	100		12		13		101		226	
New York Times FB post	165		24		29		164		382	
YouTube comments	145		10		11		144		310	
Total	410	13%	46	1%	53	2%	409	13%	918	29%
Nichols:										
CNN post on FB	68		9		3		60		140	
Fox News	123		12		12		108		255	
Rachel Nichols FB page	69		1		5		71		146	
Washington Post	108		9		3		101		221	
Total	368	12%	31	1%	23	1%	340	10%	762	24%
Totals	1,234	40%	313	10%	301	10%	1,264	40%	3,112	100%

occurrences – 100%). This means (considering the total occurrences of (im) politeness) that roughly 900 *comments* – 41% (out of 2,220 – 100% in analytic corpus) were coded for more than one combination of the above, which is not uncommon due to the polylogal nature of online commentary (Bou-Franch & Garcés-Conejos Blitvich, 2014), as it addresses a multiplicity of audiences, due to context collapse (Marwick & boyd, 2011).

Results from Tables 5 and 6 also show that it was only in a few instances that intergroup impoliteness was potentially mitigated by the concurrent use of politeness; therefore, in 921 *comments* – 42% circa half of those included in the analytic corpus, contained straightforward impoliteness toward the outgroup, whereas intragroup impoliteness was only present in 301 comments – 14% (in analytic corpus). Due to space constraints, only patterns of (im)politeness with a circa 10% (or higher) of incidence in the corpus will be discussed and illustrated in detail.

6.2.2.1 Intragroup (Im)politeness

Regarding the intragroup, the most common positive politeness strategies (Table 7) were "Presuppose/assert/raise common ground" (1,027 occurrences – 27.2%), as can be seen in Example 14 where the toxicity of Hollywood as a job-environment is taken as a given:

> Example 14
> Hollywood is the worst place to work. This is no secret. If you're successful in Hollywood's poisonous environment, it's most likely because you sold your soul to the machine or you have no soul and ARE the machine.

and, in Example 15, with a reference to "the swamp," Washington's "old and corrupt guard"

> Example 15
> She [Cheney] needs to head down to the Swamp just like the rest of them.

Ingroup members also provided detailed accounts of the thought processes behind their positively/negatively valenced assessments, thus "Give (or ask for) reasons" was highly salient (989 occurrences – 26.2%), and tried to seek, at least, partial (if not complete) agreement (388 occurrences – 10.3%) with others. This can be seen in Example 16 where, despite agreeing with the ingroup that Ellen should not be canceled, very specific reasons were provided for why she was partially to blame for her show's alleged toxic atmosphere:

Table 7 Intragroup politeness.

Intragroup politeness	Number of occurrences	Percentage of total
Presuppose-raise-assert common ground	1,027	27.2
Give (or ask for) reasons	989	26.2
State the FTA as a general rule	433	11.5
Seek agreement	388	10.3
Impersonalize S & H – Avoid pronouns I and you	212	5.6
Give gifts to H – goods, sympathy, understanding, cooperation	209	5.5
Question, hedge	174	4.6
Avoid disagreement	63	1.7
Be optimistic	54	1.4
Use ingroup identity markers	45	1.2
Offer, promise	34	0.9
Exaggerate (interest, approval, sympathy with H)	33	0.9
Include both S and H in the activity	15	0.4
Notice attends to H (interests, wants, needs, goods)	15	0.4
Be pessimistic	13	0.3
Joke	13	0.3
Give deference	11	0.3
Go on record as incurring a debt or not indebting H	10	0.3
Apologize	9	0.2
Nominalize	7	0.2
Assert presuppose S's knowledge of and concern for H's wants	6	0.2
Be conventionally indirect	4	0.1
Minimize the imposition	3	0.1
Assume or assert reciprocity	2	0.1
Intensify interest to H	2	0.1
Total	**3,771**	**100.0**

Example 16

honestly, ellen IS responsible for the culture, shes the boss. she needs to be more accessible and to show her employees that she cares. if her exec producers feared reprimand for treating employees poorly, i doubt theyd be so blatant. if she held a meeting now and then with her staff where she listens to their issues and finds solutions (that she follows through on) then i doubt upper management would feel so invincible. im not cancelling ellen, im pointing out that that workplace is the way it is bc she allows it to be

"Seek agreement" is also shown in Example 17 where it is settled that Cheney needs to behave according to the expectations of those who voted for her, not her own volition:

Example 17
A: and more of them should definitely be held accountable. They forgot who it is they work for.
B: Yep. Representatives need to be called to task more often. Not her voice, but the voice of her constituents.

Regarding the use of intragroup negative politeness, in Example 18, a Republican avoids blaming specific GOP members for Cheney's ousting and, by deploying the "State the FTA as a general rule" (443 occurrences – 11.5%), faults her whole party, alleging they have *all* lost their mind:

Example 18
Keep being a TRUE Republican!!! I have come to think that my party has lost its mind. I applaud your dedication to truth!!!!

The significant prevalence of positive politeness (63% of most frequent strategies – Table 7) is not surprising: it is commonly used for building rapport and fostering relationships, expressing solidarity and camaraderie, enhancing harmony, and eliciting cooperation and collaboration. These are all essential to the creation and maintenance of ingroups, especially to the type of light groups considered here which need to be created on the go by individuals among whom Distance (Brown & Levinson, 1987) is very high. In and outgroup(s) need to be established quickly in online free spaces and claiming, attributing, and (non)verifying identities by showering the ingroup with positive politeness is quite an effective way to do so. I would argue that positive (and to a lesser degree negative) politeness helps to quickly gel the ingroup(s), thus allowing the fast-establishing joint common ground, key to the collective intentionality of exposing, ostracizing, and so on, the different targets.

The most frequent intragroup impoliteness (Table 8) included "Pointed criticisms/complaints" (270 occurrences – 32.3%), like those lodged (Example 19), by Republicans of their own representatives,

Table 8 Intragroup impoliteness.

Intragroup impoliteness	Number of occurrences	Percentage of total
Pointed criticisms – complaints	270	32.3
Condescension	164	19.6
Disagreements	117	14.0
Unpalatable questions and or presuppositions	76	9.1
Form driven – implicated impoliteness	58	6.9
Negative expressive	54	6.5
Message enforcers	34	4.1
Convention driven – sarcasm, irony	24	2.9
Threats	20	2.4
Dismissals	16	1.9
Context driven – Bald on record	1	0.1
Silencers	1	0.1
Insults	0	0.0
Total	**835**	**100.0**

Example 19

I did the same. Registered "no party preference" because i realized, thanks to Trump AND McCarthy (my embarrassing rep) that I can't support their lies.

"Condescensions" (164 occurrences – 19%), seen in Example 20, in which each faction of a seemly divided GOP claims moral superiority:

Example 20

as a lifelong Republican I am very proud of her as well as hundreds of thousands of other Republicans who continue to leave the party that used to be what we saw as our moral compass.

and "Disagreements" (117 occurrences – 14%), often involving non-verifications of a claimed Republican identity, as illustrated in Example 21:

Example 21

A: same here a registered republican they lost and I'm only one one of thousands

B: You are not and have never been a Republican. GFYS !

Interestingly, the highest number of intragroup impoliteness occurrences (225 – 7%, versus 53 – 2% for DeGeneres, and 23 – 1% for Nichols; Table 6) were found in Cheney's files. What is at stake here is the struggle regarding what being a Republican means. It is a civil strife for full claims to/verification of the identity.

6.2.2.2 Intergroup (Im)politeness

Concerning types of intergroup politeness (Table 9), with circa a third of the total occurrences of impoliteness (280 occurrences – 26.4%), among the most used strategies was "Give (or ask for) reasons." For instance, in Example 22,

Table 9 Intergroup politeness.

Intergroup politeness	Number of occurrences	Percentage of total
Give (or ask for) reasons	280	26.4
Presuppose-raise-assert common ground	271	25.5
State the FTA as a general rule	132	12.4
Give gifts to H – goods, sympathy, understanding, cooperation	83	7.8
Seek agreement	74	7.0
Question, hedge	54	5.1
Impersonalize S & H – Avoid pronouns I and you	44	4.1
Avoid disagreement	39	3.7
Be optimistic	18	1.7
Give deference	10	0.9
Exaggerate (interest, approval, sympathy with H)	10	0.9
Offer, promise	10	0.9
Use ingroup identity markers	9	0.8
Go on record as incurring a debt or not indebting H	5	0.5
Notice, attend to H (interests, wants, needs, goods)	4	0.4
Apologize	3	0.3
Joke	3	0.3
Be conventionally indirect	2	0.2
Be pessimistic	2	0.2
Nominalize	2	0.2
Assert presuppose S's knowledge of and concern for H's wants	2	0.2
Assume or assert reciprocity	2	0.2
Include both S and H in the activity	2	0.2
Minimize the imposition	1	0.1
Intensify interest to H	0	0.0
Total	**1,062**	**100.0**

detailed justifications are given regarding why Nichols should be canceled in response to a comment that argued in her support:

Example 22

It may have been said in private, but it became public, which made her position at the network untenable. In the end, she is being let go because she criticized her network bosses and word got back to them . . . Bottom line is that the bosses do not like to be criticized. May not be fair, but that's what happens when you work for somebody else.

Across the corpus, it was observed that rather than engaging in ad hominem attacks or bare bones disqualifications of others, participants in this Big C conversation (even though criticizing or disagreeing with others' views) took care in explaining and detailing the reasons behind their own positioning. That happened in relation both to the ingroup – as discussed – and the outgroup(s), albeit with significant numerical differences: "Give (or ask for) reasons" was the second most frequently used intragroup politeness strategy (989 occurrences) and the first most frequent for intergroup politeness (280 occurrences).

"Presuppose/raise/assert common ground" (271 occurrences – 25.5%), and "State the FTA as a general rule" (132 occurrences – 12.4%) were also frequently used intergroup. The ingroup tried to find common ground, points on which to agree on, with the outgroup and show understanding and further tried to assuage potential conflict by making general, rather than specific, claims about content that may be perceived as aggressive or offensive. In Example 23, negative experiences with bosses (expected to be shared by many in the in/outgroup) are used to try to mitigate disagreement regarding Ellen's *cancelation*, also Ellen being a bad boss is presented as a general rather than a particular incident:

Example 23

I think so many people experience terrible bosses that it's not a stretch for them to come to a conclusion that Ellen could be one of them. I also know someone personally who left her show for those exact reasons, and I don't usually buy coincidences 👤

Remarkably, the highest incidence of intergroup politeness was also found in Cheney's files (236 occurrences – 8%; Table 6). This paradox in addressing both the out and ingroups further supports the difficulty in dealing with the type of fragmentation and internal conflict that the GOP is experiencing of late, thus setting the boundaries between who is *in* and who is *out*.

Table 10 Intergroup impoliteness.

Intergroup impoliteness	Number of occurrences	Percentage of total
Pointed criticisms – complaints	1,128	30.6
Condescension	650	17.6
Disagreements	457	12.4
Insults	369	10.0
Unpalatable questions and or presuppositions	366	9.9
Form driven – implicated impoliteness	234	6.3
Negative expressive	208	5.6
Convention driven – sarcasm, irony	120	3.3
Message enforcers	92	2.5
Dismissals	30	0.8
Threats	20	0.5
Silencers	13	0.4
Context driven – Bald on record	1	0.0
Total	**3,688**	**100.0**

Pertaining to intergroup impoliteness (Table 10), the most common formulae found in the corpus were "Pointed criticism/complaints" (1,128 occurrences – 30.6%) such as the negatively valenced critiques of DeGeneres in Example 24 as insensitive and Nichols as overbearing in Example 25,

> Example 24
> She took delight in the pain of some Olympic athletes, and ran them shouting in agony over and over all month, as she chortled gleefully. Hello?

> Example 25
> I thought Nichols was over bearing as a host. Never appreciated how she stepped over the voices of her co-hosts and guests.

"Condescensions" (650 occurrences – 17.6%) and different types of "Insults" (369 occurrences – 10%) were also very frequent intergroups. For instance, in Example 26, where Wyoming voters are blamed and deemed ignorant, for electing Cheney; Trump is depicted as greedy, a liar, and a grifter; and the GOP is characterized as fascist. In contrast to this condescending view, the Democrats (the ingroup) are presented as calm and dignified constitutionalists:

Example 26
WY voters listen up: this is your fault. You don't know your mouth from your posterior if you think GOP elected officials represent the people. How ignorant. Look at 45 as an example of greed, lies and graft. I bet some of you even gave him $ to fight the results of a fair election. Fascists all. Now we have Biden and Kamala who will serve with dignity and calm compared to Comrade tRumph … She is obeying her oath to uphold THE CONSTITUTION above all.

"Disagreements" (457 occurrences – 12.4%) emerged as one of the most common impoliteness intergroup manifestations, often realized along with "Condescensions" and "Insults" as we can see in Example 27, where an ESPN supporter explicitly disagreed with another commenter's interpretation:

Example 27
So back to the original comment. He said he isn't watching sports. He DID NOT say he was avoiding any and all sports related content. I guess your intellect can't quite grasp WHY people are not watching sports or WHY ESPN has lost so many viewers. By merely watching sports you contribute to their income. By reading about sports on FOX News you are only helping FOX. ESPN doesn't get a dime. Same with reading about a player or game. Now you know.

Generally, we also find similarities regarding the use of the formulae in relation to the in/outgroup, differing substantially in numeric realization of occurrences as well. A remarkable contrast between intra/intergroup impoliteness was the number of "Insults" found in the latter (369 occurrences – 10%, Table 10), compared to 0 in the former (Table 8).

The high incidence of impoliteness directed at the outgroup(s) can be related to the coercive function of impoliteness (Culpeper, 2011) which seeks the assertion of power and dominance and also to boundary-setting regarding in/outgroups, both crucial to *cancelation*. Further, by deliberately violating polite behavior, individuals may aim to provoke reactions, question established norms, or draw attention to social issues. Thus, the overt and profuse display of impoliteness is an act of positioning and, relationally, of difference from others. From this perspective, it serves as an effective group gelling mechanism and (as we will discuss below) heightens members' commitment to the group's collective intentionality.

In this respect, and relevant for this analysis is the fact that only eight occurrences (0.4% of comments in corpus) of metapragmatic assessment (Examples-28 and 29) regarding the inappropriacy of other commentators' communicative choices were found in the entire corpus.

Example 28
Good lord, some of you people really have the claws out. Try this: read
what she said again, then read your comment and see which one is full of
anger or totally inappropriate.

Example 29
my god you're rude. jesus learn some manners.

Given this very small number of occurrences, it seems that impoliteness
toward the outgroup is expected in many online public spaces: posters may
struggle discursively regarding perceptions of *cancelees, ultimate cancelers,* or other social actors' behavior but, across the board, the use of impoliteness *per se* is almost never questioned or assessed as inappropriate. This
may point to the use of impoliteness in some online public spaces having
become normative for some uses, which is quite different from offline public
spaces, in which politeness/civility is the norm (Bannister & O'Sullivan,
2013). In this sense, it could be argued that free, uncensored, unregulated
online spaces (Section 3.1) become *tyrannical spaces* (such as those offline
spaces where bullying takes place, Andrew & Chen, 2006) where, at least
part of, the degradation ceremonies, group exclusion, and ostracism related
to *cancelation* genre ecologies occur.

Politeness, however, still seems to be expected and normative in relation to the
ingroup. This synergy has been less researched and deserves more attention,
especially in the context of polylogues (but see Bou-Franch & Garcés-Conejos
Blitvich, 2014; Garcés-Conejos Blitvich & Fernandez-Amaya, 2023). In general,
this may lead us to tentatively conclude that politeness, as a means to ingroupness,
emerges as a pre-requisite for the light group's joint deployment of impoliteness.
Indeed, as Blommaert (2017a: 26) remarked regarding normativity in online
spaces, "such apparently open, highly diverse, free and unscripted communicative
spaces are very rapidly filled with ad hoc and solidified norms." The deployment of
im/politeness is a fast and effective way to create separation and debasement and
ingroupness and elevation respectively. In addition, the conveyance of (im)polite-
ness is crucially related to emotions, which will be discussed separately in the next
section although they are very often expressed simultaneously.

6.2.3 Moral Emotions

One of the key functions of (im)politeness is the expression of emotions (see
Culpeper, 2011; Garcés-Conejos Blitvich, 2009, 2013). For instance, individuals may resort to impolite language or gestures to vent their emotions and
express dissatisfaction or irritation. Conversely, feeling grateful or empathetic

can lead to expressions of politeness and appreciation. In addition, expressing negative/positive emotions may be assessed contextually as im/polite behavior. In their in-depth review of (im)politeness and emotions, Langlotz and Locher (2017) propose three areas of research regarding the intersection between pragmatics and emotions. Most relevant to this Element is sociality and emotions, that is, "[w]hat is at stake when emotions come into play (e.g., identity construction and relationship negotiations)?"

*Cancelees/ultimate cancelers/*associated ingroups/outgroups' perceived im/moral behavior may be the trigger of positive/negative (moral) emotions which are, in turn, communicated (non)linguistically. This points to morality and (im) politeness being key in social identity construction.[21] Indeed, emotions have been claimed to play a critical role in the processes whereby individuals assume cultural identities (Keltner & Haidt, 1999; Lawler, 1992; Polletta & Jasper, 2001) and in collective intentionality (Jankovic & Ludwig, 2017). More specifically, also regarding groups, shared negative emotion has been linked to group conflict, whereas collective positive emotion is seen as eliciting cooperation and higher performance (Guillory et al., 2011).

To further probe the data, the intersections between moral emotion and in/outgroup(s) were scrutinized through several related matrix coding queries. In this respect, the corpus was coded following Haidt's (2003) moral emotions taxonomy and considering how expression of said emotions were related to in/outgroup(s).

6.2.3.1 Other-Condemning Emotions

Results showed that other-condemning emotions were mostly expressed in relation to the outgroup(s), with "Contempt" being the one more frequently found in the corpus, 1,104 occurrences – 74.6%, in relation to the intergroup and 283 – 19.1% in relation to the intragroup (Table 11). This makes sense in the *cancelation* context since contempt is defined as the feeling of (usually moral) dislike for and superiority over another person, group of people, and/or their actions. Further, contempt may be used to reduce interaction with individuals perceived as not contributing in meaningful ways to the group, thus judged to be lower or less capable than the self (Hutcherson & Gross, 2011).

Regarding how it is realized, definitions of contempt further detail that treating others with disrespect and mocking them with sarcasm and condescension are forms of contempt, as are hostile humor, name-calling, mimicking, and body language such as eye-rolling and sneering. Based on this

---

[21] See Garcés-Conejos Blitvich and Kádár (2021) for a discussion of the interface between im/morality and im/politeness.

Table 11 Other-condemning emotions and in/outgroups.

	Intragroup		Intergroup		Percentage of Total	
			Other-condemning emotions			
Anger	54	3.7%	33	2.2%	87	5.9%
Contempt	1,104	74.6%	283	19.1%	1,387	93.8%
Disgust	3	0.2%	2	0.1%	5	0.3%
	1,161	78.5%	318	21.5%	1,479	100.0%

interpretation, it would be expected that contempt would be mostly realized using impoliteness formulae. Related to this context, impoliteness and negatively valenced emotions may be expressed to construct individuals and groups as nonconformist, rebellious, or unique and to position group members very clearly in opposition to the outgroup(s).

To verify these assumptions, another matrix coding query was run which showed a strong correlation between the expression of other-condemning emotions and impoliteness, more concretely "Criticism/complaints" (1,223 occurrences – 29.3%), "Condescension" (767 occurrences – 18.4%), "Disagreement" (504 occurrences – 12.1%), and "Insults" (437 occurrences – 10.5%) (Table 12). In this respect, in Examples 30, 31, and 32, "Contempt" is expressed along with "Criticism" (Republican lie, deny, deflect, and vilify; the public is gullible; ESPN treated Nichols unfairly), "Insults" and "Condescension" (despicable, RepubliCONS, undiversified, hateful, PURE BS), and "Disagreements" (it is not Democrats but Republicans who are fascists; Nichols should not have been fired) among others.

Example 30
And they're calling Democrats fascists?! The default strategy of RepubliCONS, in every situation, is to lie, deny, deflect and vilify. How can anyone vote for these despicable people?

Example 31
It's fascinating how their own hatefulness is OK because Ellen must be evil because the media and the mob have told them so. I'm no fan of Ellen but I hate this trial by social media and the mob.

Example 32
THIS IS PURE B.S.!!! RACHEL
NICHOLS WAS THE BEST THING E.S.P.N. HAD ON THEIR NETWORK EVERY SINGLE DAY REGARDING THE N.B.A., IN MY OPINION!! NOTHING THAT SHE SAID WAS OFFENSIVE TO OR ABOUT MARIA TAYLOR!! IF ANYTHING SHE CALLED OUT ESPN

Table 12 Impoliteness formulae and other-condemning emotions.

Impoliteness Formulae	Contempt		Anger		Disgust		Total	
	Occurrences	Percentage of Total	Occurrences	Percentage of Total	Occurrences	Percentage of Total	Occurrences	Percentage of Total
Pointed criticisms - Complaints	1,143	27.4%	76	1.8%	4	0.1%	1,223	29.3%
Condescensions	714	17.1%	52	1.2%	1	0.0%	767	18.4%
Disagreements	470	11.3%	31	0.7%	3	0.1%	504	12.1%
Insults	405	9.7%	28	0.7%	4	0.1%	437	10.5%
Form driven - Implicated impoliteness	370	8.9%	35	0.8%	1	0.0%	406	9.7%
Unpalatable questions and or presuppositions	231	5.5%	20	0.5%	0	0.0%	251	6.0%
Negative expressives	216	5.2%	23	0.6%	1	0.0%	240	5.8%
Convention driven - sarcasm, irony	130	3.1%	2	0.0%	1	0.0%	133	3.2%
Message enforcers	94	2.3%	7	0.2%	0	0.0%	101	2.4%
Threats	37	0.9%	13	0.3%	0	0.0%	50	1.2%
Dismissals	36	0.9%	6	0.1%	0	0.0%	42	1.0%
Silencers	12	0.3%	3	0.1%	0	0.0%	15	0.4%
Context driven - Bald on record	2	0.0%	0	0.0%	0	0.0%	2	0.0%
Totals	3,860	92.5%	296	7.1%	15	0.4%	4,171	100.0%

FOR THEIR LACK OF DIVERSITY!! EVERYONE SHOULD BOYCOTT ESPN NBA COVERAGE THAT IS SLOTTED IN TO REPLACE RACHEL NICHOLS' & "THE JUMP!" 😠😠😡😡😡😡😡😡

In view of the results, it seems important to try to account for why further offense is considered a moral and fair retribution to perceived offense, a kind of *reactive aggression* (Allen & Anderson, 2017). In a highly moralizing context, such as *cancelation*, expressing other-condemning emotions may be a way for groups to signal their moral quality to others. Another way to explain it is by recourse to "the dark side of morality" (Monroe & Ashby Plant, 2019; Rempala et al., 2020). This concept refers to instances in which our deeply held moral convictions serve as justification for actions that are usually deemed morally impermissible, such as engaging in collective violence with the goal to regulate social relationships, as in the case with *cancelation*. Moral convictions do not only regulate the self, but also what others ought to do. As Workman et al. (2020: 2) claim: "When the morally convicted are confronted with societal attitudes out of sync with their moral values, some may find this sufficiently intolerable to justify violence against those who challenge their beliefs." This violence may range in scope from the display of aggressive communicative behavior (as we have observed in the corpus) to the bombing of abortion clinics. In the present case, *cancelees', ultimate cancelers'* behavior is seen as morally reprehensible; the morally convicted see themselves, therefore, justified in exposing *them* to show who they "really" are, make them face consequences for their actions (legal, financial) and – also aiming at social regulation – try to dissuade others from displaying similar behavior or risk being similarly exposed. In this sense, the dark side of morality is closely connected to degradation ceremonies (Section 6.2.1).

6.2.3.2 Suffering

Important as well is the very similar number of total occurrences (1,258 – 100%; Table 13) of another emotion family, also other-directed, which encompasses sympathy and compassion. Sympathy is defined as an emotional response that involves both understanding and being moved by another's suffering/joy. Compassion adds to this the motivation to relieve that suffering. Results showed that the highest percentage of suffering emotions was directed intragroup (979 occurrences – 77.8%).

Given the nature of the suffering family, it was anticipated that its linguistic realization would be strongly linked to politeness, especially positive politeness due to its emphasis on social bonding and affiliation. The results of another matrix coding query confirmed this prediction as three of the four most common politeness strategies deployed to express suffering are positive in orientation

Table 13 Suffering emotions.

Suffering emotions	Sympathy/Compassion	
	Number of occurrences	Percentage of total
Intergroup	279	22.2
Intragroup	979	77.8
	1,258	100.0

("Presuppose/raise/assert common ground" 861 occurrences – 26.4%; "Give (or ask for) reasons," 850 occurrences – 26.1%; and "Seek agreement" 321 occurrences – 9.8%). The remaining one, "State the FTA as a general rule," 369 occurrences – 11.3%) is a negative politeness strategy. (Table 14).

For instance, in Examples 33 and 34, suffering emotions are expressed via an array of politeness strategies, such as "Raise/assert/presuppose common ground" (we both were raised Christian Scientists, we are fellow Republicans), "Give (or ask for) reasons" (Ellen lives by religious principles, Cheney deserves respect because she is courageous); "State the FTA as a general rule" (People just love to hate a good person); "Notice, attend to H (interests, wants, needs, goods)," (I respect your courage; Keeping spreading love):

Example 33
Ellen was raised as a Christian Scientist by her family and so was I. We are no longer Christian Scientists, but I can still see that Ellen uses principles of that religion in her life – love, inclusiveness, wholeness, spirit. You cannot find fault with Ellen. People just love to hate a good person! Keep at the love, Ellen!!

Example 34
I just wanted to say, as a fellow Republican, that I respect the fact that you did the right thing knowing what the consequences could be.

As in the case of (im)politeness, the presence of positively valenced emotions is not necessarily expected when analyzing instantiations of *cancelation*. This may be because milder emotions, contrary to negative ones, do not have as a strong potential for disrupting or motivating online inter/intragroup communication (Guillory et al., 2011) and are, therefore, less focused on. In general, for (non)researchers, there seems to be a negative bias whereby individuals tend to pay more attention to negative stimuli. However, displaying positive emotions toward the ingroup plays a crucial role in gelling the group quickly by showing others you feel like they do.

Table 14 Suffering emotions and politeness.

Politeness strategies	Sympathy/ compassion occurrences	Percentage of total
Presuppose-raise-assert common ground	861	26.4
Give or ask for reasons	850	26.1
State the FTA as a general rule	369	11.3
Seek agreement	321	9.8
Give gifts to H – goods, sympathy, understanding, cooperation	222	6.8
Impersonalize S & H – avoid pronouns I and you	165	5.1
Question, hedge	154	4.7
Be optimistic	56	1.7
Avoid disagreement	56	1.7
Exaggerate (interest, approval, sympathy with H)	38	1.2
Use ingroup identity markers	34	1.0
Offer, promise	32	1.0
Notice, attend to H (interests, wants, needs, goods)	15	0.5
Include both S and H in the activity	13	0.4
Give deference	12	0.4
Joke	11	0.3
Apologize	10	0.3
Go on record as incurring a debt or not indebting H	10	0.3
Be pessimistic	8	0.2
Assert presuppose S's knowledge of and concern for H's wants	7	0.2
Nominalize	7	0.2
Assume or assert reciprocity	3	0.1
Minimize the imposition	2	0.1
Intensify interest to H	2	0.1
Be conventionally indirect	1	0.0
Totals	3,259	100.0

To find this duality of emotions is not exceptional, however. Jasper (2012) suggests that rather than humans just experiencing a single emotion at a time, emotions tend to combine in "moral batteries." These emotional pairings are at the core of agency (Jasper, 2012). Thus, moral batteries indicate a direction for action: away from the unappealing state toward the appealing one. One of those moral batteries seems to be intergroup other-condemning/intragroup suffering as shown in the corpus. Despite their differences, what both the other-condemning and suffering emotion families have in common is that they underlie mobilization. As Jasper (2012: 37) argues: "This dynamic is like a moral–emotional battery that, by separating positive and negative charges, gives us a shock— some energy that can help move us. It is the contrast between the positive and the negative states of affairs that propels us, or at least captures our imagination."

Further interpreting these results from an emotional geographies' perspective (Davidson et al., 2005), it can be argued that online free spaces where *cancelation* occurs emerge as other-condemning/suffering (Haidt, 2003) emotional spaces where behavior is assessed as morally deficient and, in turn, aggressively evaluated. The dynamic between condemning the outgroup and suffering for the ingroup is central to site normativity and to group mobilization, entitativity, and agency.

7 Conclusions

The aim of this Element was twofold. It involved an in-depth investigation of *CC* from a discursive-pragmatic perspective and, concurrently, the establishment of the bases for pragmatics/(im)politeness research to address intergroup communication more meaningfully. This was possible because *CC*, in addition to its inherent interest and complexity, provides a quintessential example of intergroup communication.

The theoretical chapters of the Element approached potential ways to circumvent the hurdles to a pragmatics/(im)politeness of groups by proposing to make it more discursive in orientation and by paying close attention to the interrelation of the macro/meso/micro-levels of analysis. Out of the three, the meso-level emerged as key as it is the level of practices and, as such, of groups. Drawing from Fairclough's (2003) discourse model (with some reformulations, Fairclough, 2004; Pennycook, 2010), genre practices and their interconnections and amalgamations were seen as fundamental units to help analysts tease out the role of context in interaction. Identity (social/groupal), as a core concept of discourses/genres enacted via style practices and (re)entextualized in texts, and its synergetic relationship with face is viewed as crucial, along with the need to consider collective intentionality when theorizing groups. Special attention was given to the symbiosis between online spaces, their affordances, and group formation. Off/online spaces, where *cancelation* is carried out, were seen, in geo-semiotics and emotional geographies terms, as historical, political, tied to emotions, and crucially related to normativity and group entitativity and agency.

The empirical chapters, in turn, offered a three-layered analysis of the macro/ meso/micro realizations of *CC*. Despite its ubiquity and recognizability, most research on *CC* to date has focused on the macro-level. This has resulted, in my view, in partial analyses and incomplete conceptualizations of this socio-cultural phenomenon. To answer RQ1, how can *CC* be conceptualized at the macro-level? – a thorough review of the available archival, (non)academic, and statistical sources and the application of Discourse-inspired concepts resulted into *CC* being envisioned as a Big C Conversation. In this regard, *CC* is associated with liberal-leaning/disenfranchised groups' accessing public discourse to retake power from those who have traditionally held it and engage in discussions about morality. A more recent understanding is that of *CC* being weaponized by the Right, equated to political correctness, an attempt to try to silence those who dissent from liberal views, and led by frenzied *woke* mobs. A close analysis of the data, at the micro-level, problematizes these neat distinctions and presents a more fractured view of *CC*. In addition, with very few notable exceptions (Saint-Louis, 2021), extant literature has conflated *CC* with the practice of *cancelation*, a proper meso-level phenomenon.

The next part of the analysis sought to answer RQ2 – What genre, meso-level, practices are involved in *cancelation*? – and drew insights from the general analysis of the *cancelation* cases included in from the *CC Corpus* and, more specifically, on Cheney's, DeGeneres', and Nichols'. No study, to my knowledge, had delved into the intricacies of the very complex practices involved in *cancelation*. Drawing from genre theory, more specifically work on genre ecologies, *cancelation* was described as the ad hoc assemblages of very diverse off/online (non)occluded genres (which vary substantially from case to case) out of which the online comment genre emerged as, what may be argued is, a sine qua non condition for *cancelation* and was, therefore, selected to be the focus of the micro-level analysis. Despite this centrality, the meso-level analysis clearly established that *CC* is not just a collective endeavor or an online phenomenon, but a hybrid mixture of light and thick groups led by collective intentionality, and a veritable example of the on/offline nexus.

An in-depth qualitative analysis of a sizeable corpus, 2,200 comments extracted from diverse platforms to maximize inclusivity of viewpoints was probed, with the help of NVivo 1.6.1, to answer RQ3 and RQ3.1: How is *cancelation* realized at the micro-level? (with a focus on online practices); and, how do the micro-level resources used contribute to the light groups involved in *cancelation* becoming agents? Micro-level analyses of *cancelation* are very scarce but necessary (Ng, 2020) because, just as at the meso-level, micro-level results problematize general, extant views on *CC*. Findings showed that *CC* has certainly evolved by aiming at different targets, either the *cancelee*, the *ultimate canceler*, or both. However, none of these types can be clearly ascribed to a political persuasion, as would be expected from the description of the first and second waves of *CC*. Indeed, both the liberal/conservative leaning participate in the three distinct *cancelation* processes found in the corpus. What all three types had in common, however, was their ability to be accounted for in terms of *degradation ceremonies* associated with identity reduction and stigmatization as a result of perceived moral failings. Once targets are reduced to one-dimensional, immoral beings and positioned as outsiders, ostracism and aggressive retaliation are seen as justified. In this sense, online spaces may be akin to tyrannical spaces, where bullying and other group exclusion practices can take place. However, this picture is quite distinct from the one that painted *CC* as led by a unidirectional mob: if *cancelers* should be thought of as mobs, there is certainly more than one involved, often working contrariwise, albeit each being led by a collectively embraced goal.

Mainstream *CC* research and the present analysis of the meso-level coincided in highlighting the role of online groups as initiators and continuators of *cancelation*. This efficacy requires for groups to have achieved entitativity and agency. Traditionally, it is thick groups that have been considered agents. Light groups have received less attention and whether they can become agents has not often been addressed. The micro-level part of the present analysis sought to unveil the interactional resources [(im)politeness and the expression of emotions, both often mentioned in descriptions of *CC*] used in *cancelation* and whether these could be related to the gelling and concomitant agency of the groups involved. Results, not necessarily expected as mainstream *CC* has characterized the phenomenon as punitive and its realizations as aggressive, unveiled two key synergies that could be related to the construction of group agency. Regarding the first, impoliteness (given the extant descriptions of *CC*) was expected and was present in the corpus directed mostly intergroup; politeness (generally positive-face and intragroup oriented) was certainly not but had, however, an almost equal number of occurrences. Profuse positive politeness manifestations were interpreted as a clear and quick ingroup-building mechanism and a necessary step toward the deploying of impoliteness toward the outgroup. Impoliteness, for its part, was related to its coercive function, to the wielding of power, and establishing who is *in* or *out* of the group. (Im)politeness also has a salient emotional function. In this context, per the descriptions of *CC*, the expectations were that those emotions would be moral in nature and mostly included in the other-condemning family. This was certainly the case, but just as in in the case of (im)politeness, results were somewhat unexpected. Along with the expression of other-condemning emotions, especially outgroup-directed contempt, the emotions included in the suffering family, directed at the ingroup, had a strong presence. Batteries of emotions such (other-condemning/suffering) have been related to action and mobilization, as well as a strong group gelling mechanism: associating with those who feel the same way you do feels like a safe option. It is the combination of the digital free space (described as other-condemning/suffering, following the tenets of emotional geographies) and its affordances, together with the managing of relationships via (im)politeness and the sharing of emotional investment and common goals that seem to turn the light groups participating in *cancelation* into group agents.

As detailed in Section 4, the *cancelation* genre ecologies launched against Cheney, DeGeneres, and Nichols achieved their goals. However, how permanent the consequences of *cancelation* are remains doubtful; Nichols is gainfully employed by Showtime Basketball and DeGeneres returned with a show "About time for yourself . . . with Ellen," a comedy web-based short series that debuted on her YouTube channel in October 2022. For her part, Cheney – although having received various accolades such as being one of the 2022 recipients of the John F. Kennedy Profile in Courage Award, for bravery in protecting and defending democracy – is not likely to return to politics soon (as long as Trump remains in control of the Republican party). Regarding the *ultimate cancelers*, ESPN has experienced a significant decrease in subscribers and NBC's viewership has also declined; however, this downward trend is not uncommon among different television formats and shows, as new generations migrate to digital media for all their informative and recreational needs and cannot be causally attributed to potential boycotts triggered by *cancelation*. The GOP did not experience the significant gains they expected in the 2022 mid-term elections – how much of this can be traced back to the Cheney-effect is hard to gauge – but at the time of writing, Trump is the leading candidate for the 2024 GOP presidential nomination.

Although *CC* has evolved quickly, it could be argued that most *cancelers* are aware that the consequences of *cancelation* may be ephemeral, at least for some targets. This begs the question of why *cancelations* are still so prevalent. One possible explanation is that participating in them is performative, ritualistic, that is, actions displayed for the audience where the focus is mostly on the process rather than the outcome (Lewis & Christin, 2022; Watson-Jones & Legare, 2016). Interestingly for this discussion, both performance/rituals have been strongly connected to identifying with, committing to, and strengthening group values. This shows that, regardless of how *CC* may be construed, it is first and foremost an intergroup phenomenon: a type of socio-cultural phenomenon that needs to be tackled from an inter-group perspective. In this Element, I have tried to take some first steps toward a pragmatics/(im)politeness approach to intergroup communication. Certainly, much more research is needed in this regard, and it is my hope that this Element will help inspire it.

References

Addeo, F., Delli Paoli, A., Esposito, M. & Bolcato, M. (2019). Doing social research on online communities: The benefits of netnography. *Athens Journal of Social Sciences*, 7(1), 9–38.

Al-Gharbi, M. (2022).No, America is not on the brink of a civil war. *The Guardian*, 27. www.theguardian.com/commentisfree/2022/jan/27/no-america-is-not-on-the-cusp-of-a-civil-war.

Allen, J. & Anderson, C. (2017). Aggression and violence: Definitions and distinctions. In P. Sturmey, ed., *The Wiley Handbook of Violence and Aggression*. John Wiley & Sons, pp. 1–14.

Andrews, G. & Chen, S. (2006). The production of tyrannical space. *Children's Geographies*, 4(2), 239–250.

Androutsopoulos, J. (2021). Polymedia in interaction. *Pragmatics and Society*, 12(5), 707–724.

Androutsopoulos, J. & Tereick, J. (2015). YouTube: Language and discourse practices in participatory culture. In A. Georgakopoulou & T. Spilioti, eds., *The Routledge Handbook of Language and Digital Communication*. Routledge, pp. 354–370.

Angouri, J. (2015). Online communities and communities of practice. In A. Georgakopoulou & T. Spilioti, eds., *The Routledge Handbook of Language and Digital Communication*. Routledge, pp. 323–338.

Angouri, J. & Locher, M. A. (2012). Theorising disagreement. *Journal of Pragmatics*, 44(12), 1549–1553.

Appadurai, A. (1996). *Modernity at Large: Cultural Dimensions of Globalization*. University of Minnesota Press.

Ariff, Z. (2012). Ethnographic discourse analysis: Conversion to Islam ceremony. *Discourse & Communication*, 6(3), 295–322.

Arundale, R. B. (1999). An alternative model and ideology of communication for an alternative to politeness theory. *Pragmatics*, 9(1), 119–153.

Au, A. (2017). Collective identity, organization, and public reaction in protests: A qualitative case study of Hong Kong and Taiwan. *Social Sciences*, 6(4), 150, 1–17.

Bannister, J. & O'Sullivan, A. (2013). Civility, community cohesion and anti-social behaviour: Policy and social harmony. *Journal of Social Policy*, 42(1), 91–110.

Barker, C. & Galasinski, D. (2001). *Cultural Studies and Discourse Analysis: A Dialogue on Language and Identity*. Sage.

Barnhizer, D. (2021)."*Un-Canceling*" *America.*

Barron, A. & Schneider, K. P. (2014). Discourse pragmatics: Signposting a vast field. In A. Barron & K. P. Schneider, eds., *Pragmatics of Discourse.* Walter de Gruyter, pp. 1–33.

Bazerman, C. (1994). Systems of genre and the enactment of social intentions. In A. Freedman & P. Medway, eds., *Genre and the New Rhetoric.* Taylor & Francis, pp. 79–99.

Bazerman, C. (1997). The life of genre, the life in the classroom. In Bishop, W., Ostrom, H., eds., *Genre and Writing: Issues, Arguments, Alternatives.* Heinemann, Portsmouth, NH, pp. 19–26.

Bella, S. (2009). Invitations and politeness in Greek: The age variable. *Journal of Politeness Research*, 5, 243–271.

Benson, P. (2017). *The Discourse of YouTube: Multimodal Text in a Global Context.* Routledge.

Berkenkotter, C. & Huckin, T. (1993). Rethinking genre from a sociocognitive perspective. *Written Communication*, 10(4), 475–509.

Bhatia, V. K. (2015). Critical genre analysis: Theoretical preliminaries. *HERMES-Journal of Language and Communication in Business*, 27(54), 9–20.

Bhatia, V. K. (2002). Applied genre analysis: Analytical advances and pedagogical procedures. In A. M. Johns, ed., *Genre in the Classroom: Multiple Perspectives.* Lawrence Erlbaum Associates, pp. 279–283.

Blommaert, J. (2008). Artefactual ideologies and the textual production of African languages. *Language & Communication*, *28*(4), 291–307.

Blommaert, J. (2013). *Ethnography, Superdiversity and Linguistic Landscapes: Chronicles of Complexity.* Multilingual Matters.

Blommaert, J. (2017a). Durkheim and the internet: On sociolinguistics and the sociological imagination. *Tilburg Papers in Culture Studies*, 173, 1–90.

Blommaert, J. (2017b). Ludic membership and orthopractic mobilization: On slacktivism and all that. *Tilburg Papers in Culture Studies*, 193, 1–7.

Blommaert, J. (2017c). Online-offline modes of identity and community: Elliot Rodger's twisted world of masculine victimhood. *Tilburg Papers in Culture Studies*, 200, 1–10.

Blommaert, J. (2019). Political discourse in post-digital societies. *Tilburg Papers in Culture Studies*, 236, 1–10.

Blommaert, J., Smits, L. & Yacoubi, N. (2018). Context and its complications. *Tilburg Papers in Cultural Studies*, 208, 1–20.

Blommaert, J. & Varis, P. (2015). Conviviality and collectives on social media: Virality, memes, and new social structures. *Multilingual Margins*, 2(1), 31–45.

Blum-Kulka, S., House, J. & Kasper, G. (eds.). (1989). *Cross-cultural Pragmatics: Requests and Apologies*. Ablex.

Bonilla, Y. & Rosa, J. (2015). # Ferguson: Digital protest, hashtag ethnography, and the racial politics of social media in the United States. *American Ethnologist*, 42(1), 4–17.

Bou-Franch, P. & Garcés-Conejos Blitvich, P. (2014). Conflict management in massive polylogues: A case study from YouTube. *Journal of Pragmatics*, 73, 19–36.

Bousfield, D. (2008). *Impoliteness in Interaction*. John Benjamins.

Bouvier, G. (2020). Racist call-outs and cancel culture on Twitter: The limitations of the platform's ability to define issues of social justice. *Discourse, Context & Media*, 38, 100431, 1–11.

Brown, P. (1980). How and why are women more polite: Some evidence from a Mayan community. In S. McConnell-Ginet, R. Borker and N. Furman, eds., *Women and Language in Literature and Society*. Praeger, pp. 111–136.

Brown, P. & Levinson, S. (1987). *Politeness: Some Universals in Language Usage*. Cambridge University Press.

Bucholtz, M. & Hall, K. (2005). Identity and interaction: A socio-cultural linguistic approach. *Discourse Studies*, 7(4/5), 585–614.

Burke, P. & Stets, J. (2009). *Identity Theory*. Oxford University Press.

Butler, J. (1990). *Gender Trouble: Feminism and the Subversion of Identity*. Routledge.

Castells, M. (1996). *The Rise of the Network Society, the Information Age: Economy, Society and Culture*. Blackwell.

Chen, C. W. (2020). Analyzing online comments: A language-awareness approach to cultivating digital literacies. *Computer Assisted Language Learning*, 33(4), 435–454.

Cheney-Lippold, J. (2017). *We are Data*. New York University Press.

Citron, D. K. (2014). *Hate Crimes in Cyberspace*. Harvard University Press.

Clark, M. (2020). DRAG THEM: A brief etymology of so-called "cancel culture." *Communication and the Public*, 5(3/4), 88–92.

Cook, C. L., Patel, A., Guisihan, M. & Wohn, D. Y. (2021). Whose agenda is it anyway: An exploration of cancel culture and political affiliation in the United States . *SN Social Sciences*, 1(9), 237.

Costea, A. (2017). The online resources of contemporary social revolutions: The case of the Romanian #Rezist revolution. *Tilburg Papers in Culture Studies*, 190, 1–70.

Coupland, N. (2010). *Style: Language Variation and Identity*. Cambridge University Press.

Culpeper, J. (2011). *Impoliteness: Using Language to Cause Offence.* Cambridge University Press.

Culpeper, J. (2016). Impoliteness strategies. In A. Capone & J. L. Mey, eds., *Interdisciplinary Studies in Pragmatics, Culture and Society.* Springer, pp. 421–445.

Culpeper, J. (2021). Sociopragmatics: Roots and definitions. In M. Haugh, D. Z. Kádár & M. Terkourafi, eds., *The Cambridge Handbook of Sociopragmatics.* Cambridge University Press, pp. 15–29.

Culpeper, J. & Haugh, M. (2021). (Im) politeness and sociopragmatics. In M. Haugh, D. Kádár & M. Terkourafi, eds., *The Cambridge Handbook of Sociopragmatics.* Cambridge University Press, pp. 315–339.

Crockett, M. J. (2017). Moral outrage in the digital age. *Nature Human Behaviour*, 1(11), 769–771.

Davidson, J., Bondi, L. & Smith, M. (eds.). (2005). *Emotional Geographies.* Ashgate.

Davidson, J., Smith, M. & Bondi, L. (eds.). (2012). *Emotional Geographies.* Ashgate.

Davies, B. L., Merrison, A. J., & Haugh, M. (2011). *Situated Politeness.* Bloomsbury.

De Beaugrande, Robert (2011). Text linguistics. In J. Zienkowski. J. Verschueren, and J. Östman, eds., *Discursive Pragmatics.* John Benjamins Publishing Company, pp. 286–296.

Dryzek, J. (2007). Theory, evidence, and the tasks of deliberation. In S. Rosenberg, ed., *Deliberation, Participation, and Democracy: Can the People Govern?* Palgrave Macmillan, pp. 237–250.

Duchi, F. (2021). The "call-out culture" controversy: An identity-based cultural conflict. file:///C:/Users/tblit/Downloads/The_call_out_culture_controversy_An_iden%20(1).pdf.

Fahey, J., Roberts, J. & Utych, S. (2023). Principled or partisan? The effect of cancel culture framings on support for free speech. *American Politics Research*, 51(1), 69–75.

Fairclough, N. (2003). *Analysing Discourse: Textual Analysis for Social Research.* Routledge.

Fairclough, N. (2004). Semiotic aspects of social transformation and learning. In A. Rogers, ed., *An Introduction to Critical Discourse Analysis in Education.* Lawrence Erlbaum, pp. 225–235.

Fereday, J. & Muir-Cochrane, E. (2006). Demonstrating rigor using thematic analysis: A hybrid approach of inductive and deductive coding and theme development. *International Journal of Qualitative Methods*, 5(1), 80–92.

Fine, G. (2012). Group culture and the interaction order: Local sociology on the meso-level. *Annual Review of Sociology*, 38, 159–179.

Fine, G. & Hallett, T. (2014). Group cultures and the everyday life of organizations: Interaction orders and meso-analysis. *Organization Studies*, 35(12), 1773–1792.

Foucault, M. (1996). Madness only exists in society. In S. Lotringer, ed., *Foucault Live: Interviews, 1961–84*, 2nd ed. Semiotext(e) Foreign Agents Series, pp. 7–9.

Frobenius, M. & Gerhardt, C. (2017). Discourse and organization. In C. R. Hoffmann and W. Bublitz, eds., *Pragmatics of Social Media*. De Gruyter Mouton, pp. 245–273.

Garcés-Conejos Blitvich, P. (2009). Impoliteness and identity in the American news media: The culture wars. *Journal of Politeness Research*, 5, 273–304.

Garcés-Conejos Blitvich, P. (2010a). The YouTubification of politics, impoliteness and polarization. In R. Taiwo, ed., *Handbook of Research on Discourse Behavior and Digital Communication: Language Structures and Social Interaction*. IGI Global, pp. 540–563.

Garcés-Conejos Blitvich, P. (2010b). Introduction: The status quo and quo vadis of impoliteness research. *Intercultural Pragmatics*, 7(4), 535–559.

Garcés-Conejos Blitvich, P. (2010c). A genre approach to the study of im-politeness. *International Review of Pragmatics*, 2(1), 46–94.

Garcés-Conejos Blitvich, P. (2013). Introduction: Face, identity and (im)politeness. Looking backward, moving forward: From Goffman to practice theory. *Journal of Politeness Research*, 9(1), 1–33.

Garcés-Conejos Blitvich, P. (2021). Getting into the mob: A netnographic, case-study approach to online public shaming. In M. Johansson, S. Tanskanen & J. Chovanec, eds., *Analysing Digital Discourse: Between Convergence and Controversy*. Palgrave Macmillan, pp. 247–274.

Garcés-Conejos Blitvich, P. (2022a). *Karen*: Stigmatized social identity and face-threat in the on/offline nexus. *Journal of Pragmatics*, 188, 14–30.

Garcés-Conejos Blitvich, P. (2022b). Moral emotions, good moral panics, social regulation, and online public shaming. *Language & Communication*, 84, 61–75.

Garcés-Conejos Blitvich, P. & Fernández-Amaya, L. (2023). The offline/online nexus and public spaces: Morality, civility, and aggression in the attribution and ratification of the Karen social identity. In A. Parini & F. Yus, eds., *The Discursive Construction of Place in the Digital Age*. Routledge, pp. 121–151.

Garcés-Conejos Blitvich, P. & Georgakopoulou, A. (2021). Analyzing identity. In M. Haugh, D. Kádár & M. Terkourafi, eds., *The Cambridge Handbook of Sociopragmatics*. Cambridge University Press, pp. 293–314.

Garcés-Conejos Blitvich, P. & Kádár, D. (2021). Morality in sociopragmatics. In M. Haugh, D. Kádár & M. Terkourafi, eds., *The Cambridge Handbook of Sociopragmatics*. Cambridge University Press, pp. 385–407.

Garcés-Conejos Blitvich, P. & Lorenzo-Dus, N. (2022). "Go ahead and 'debunk' truth by calling it a conspiracy theory": The discourse construction of conspiracy theory theoryness in online affinity spaces. In M. Demata, V. Zorzi & A. Zottola, eds.,*Conspiracy Theory Discourses*. John Benjamins, pp. 71–98.

Garcés-Conejos Blitvich, P. & Sifianou, M. (2017). Im/politeness and identity. In J. Culpeper, M. Haugh, & D. Kádár, eds., *The Palgrave Handbook of Linguistic (Im)Politeness*. London: Palgrave MacMillan, pp. 227–256.

Garcés-Conejos Blitvich, P. & Sifianou, M. (2019). (Im)politeness and discursive pragmatics. *Journal of Pragmatics*, 145, 91–101.

Garfinkel, H. (1956). Conditions of successful degradation ceremonies. *American Journal of Sociology*, 61(5), 420–424.

Garfinkel, H. (2002). *Ethnomethodology's Program: Working out Durkheim's Aphorism*. Rowman & Littlefield Publishers.

Gee, J. P. (2005). *An Introduction to Discourse Analysis: Theory and Method*. 2nd ed. Routledge.

Gee, J. P. (2014). *How to Do Discourse Analysis: A Toolkit*. 2nd ed. Routledge.

Geertz, C. (1973). *The Interpretation of Cultures*. Basic books.

Gençer, H. (2019). Group dynamics and behaviour. *Universal Journal of Educational Research*, 7(1), 223–229.

Gilbert, M. (1989). *On Social Facts*. Routledge.

Giles, H. (ed.). (2012). *The Handbook of Intergroup Communication*. Routledge.

Goffman, E. (1959). *The Presentation of Self in Everyday Life*. Garden City.

Goffman, E. (1961). *Encounters: Two Studies in the Sociology of Interaction*. Ravenio Books.

Goffman, E. (1963a). *Stigma: Notes on the Management of Spoiled Identity*. Simon and Schuster.

Goffman, E. (1963b). *Behavior in Public Places*. The Free Press.

Goffman, E. (1955/1967). *Interaction Ritual: Essays on Face-to-Face Behaviour*. Pantheon Books.

Goldman, L. M. (2015). Trending now: The use of social media websites in public shaming punishments. *American Criminal Law Review*, 52, 415–451.

Guillory, J., Spiegel, J., Drislane, M. et al. (2011). "Upset now?" Emotion contagion in distributed groups. In Grinter, R. Rodden, T., Aoki, P., Cutrell, E., Jeffries, R. & Olson, G., eds., *Proceedings of the SIGCHI Conference on Human Factors in Computing Systems*. Association for Computing Machinery, pp. 745–748.

Haidt, J. (2003). The moral emotions. In R. Davidson, ed., *Handbook of Affective Sciences*. Oxford University Press, pp. 852–870.

Haidt, J. (2012). *The Righteous Mind: Why Good People are Divided by Politics and Religion*. Vintage.

Hatfield, H. & Hahn, J. W. (2014). The face of others: Triadic and dyadic interactions in Korea and the United States. *Journal of Politeness Research*, 10(2), 221–245.

Harrington, B., & Fine, G. A. (2000). Opening the "Black Box": Small groups and twenty-first-century sociology. *Social Psychology Quarterly*, 63(4), 312–323. https://doi.org/10.2307/2695842.

Harris, S. (2001). Being politically impolite: Extending politeness theory to adversarial political discourse. *Discourse & Society*, 12(4), 451–472.

Harmon, A. H. & Metaxas, P. T. (2010). How to create a smart mob: Understanding a social network capital. In *IADIS Int. Conf. e-Democracy, Equity and Social Justice*. https://pdfs.semanticscholar.org/21fb/133c04822d9681261 3febfdc9198d737e5ff.pdf.

Haugh, M. (2007). The discursive challenge to politeness research: An interactional alternative. *Journal of Politeness Research*, 3(2), 95–317.

Haugh, M. (2008a). Intention in pragmatics. *Intercultural Pragmatics*, 5(2), 99–110.

Haugh, M. (2008b). The place of intention in the interactional achievement of implicature. In I. Kecskés and J. Mey, eds., *Intention, Common Ground and the Egocentric Speaker-hearer*. Mouton de Gruyter, pp. 45–86.

Haugh, M. (2022). (Online) public denunciation, public incivilities and offence. *Language & Communication*, 87, 44–59.

Haugh, M. & Jaszczolt, K. (2012). Speaker intentions and intentionality. In K. Allan & K. Jaszczolt, eds., *The Cambridge Handbook of Pragmatics*. Cambridge University Press, pp. 87–112.

Haugh, M., Kádár, D. & Mills, S. (2013). Interpersonal pragmatics: Issues and debates. *Journal of Pragmatics*, 58, 1–11.

Holland, D. & Lave, J. (eds.). (2001). *History in Person*. School of American Research Press.

Holmes, J. (2013). *Women, Men and Politeness*. Routledge.

Hoover, J. & Milner, C. (1998). Rituals of humiliation and exclusion. *Reaching Today's Youth: The Community Circle of Caring Journal*, 3(1), 28–32.

Hutcherson, C. & Gross, J. (2011). The moral emotions: A social–functionalist account of anger, disgust, and contempt. *Journal of Personality and Social Psychology*, 100(4), 719–737.

Ide, S. (1989). Formal forms and discernment: Two neglected aspects of universals of linguistic politeness. *Multilingua*, 8(2/3), 223–248.

Jankovic, M. & Ludwig, K. (eds.). (2017). *The Routledge Handbook of Collective intentionality.* Routledge

Jasper, J. M. (2012). Choice points, emotional batteries, and other ways to find strategic agency at the micro-level. *Strategies for Social Change.* University of Minnesota Press, 23–42.

Jones, R. (2017). *Spoken Discourse.* Bloomsbury.

Jones, R. & Themistocleous, C. (2022). *Introducing Language and Society.* Cambridge University Press.

Joos, M. (1967). *The Five Clocks.* Harcourt, Brace and World.

Joseph, J. E. (2013). Identity work and face work across linguistic and cultural boundaries. *Journal of Politeness Research*, 9(1), 35–54.

Juliano, S. (2012). Superheroes, bandits, and cyber-nerds: Exploring the history and contemporary development of the vigilante. *Journal of International Commercial Law and Technology*, 7, 44–64.

Jurgenson, N. (2011). Digital dualism versus augmented reality. *The Society Pages*, 24, 1–2.

Kaufmann, E. (2022). The new culture wars: Why critical race theory matters more than cancel culture. *Social Science Quarterly*, 103(4), 773–788.

Keltner, D. & Haidt, J. (1999). Social functions of emotions at four levels of analysis. *Cognition & Emotion*, 13(5), 505–521.

Kemmis, S. (2009). Action research as a practice-based practice. *Educational Action Research*, *17*(3), 463–474.

Langlotz, A. & Locher, M. (2017). (Im)politeness and emotion. In J. Culpeper, M. Haugh & D. Kádár, eds., *The Palgrave Handbook of Linguistic (Im) politeness*. Palgrave Macmillan, pp. 287–322.

Lakoff, R. (1975). *Language and Woman's Place.* Harper & Row Publishers.

Lakoff, R. (1989). The limits of politeness: Therapeutic and courtroom discourse. *Multilingua*, 8(2/3), 101–129.

Lawler, E. J. (1992). Affective attachments to nested groups: A choice-process theory. *American Sociological Review*, 57(3), 327–339.

Lazarus, S. (2017). Cyber mobs: A model for improving protections for Internet users. Master's Thesis, Utica College.

Leech, G. (1983). *Principles of Pragmatics.* Longman.

Lemke, J. L. (2002). Travels in hypermodality. *Visual Communication*, 1(3), 299–325.

Lewis, R. & Christin, A. (2022). Platform drama: "Cancel culture," celebrity, and the struggle for accountability on YouTube. *New Media & Society*, 24(7), 1632–1656.

Li, H., & Jung, S. (2018). Networked audiences and cultural globalization. *Sociology Compass*, 12(4), e12570.

List, C. & Pettit, P. (2011). *Group Agency: The Possibility, Design, and Status of Corporate Agents*. Oxford University Press.

Locher, M. (2008). Relational work, politeness and identity construction. In G. Antos & E. Ventola, eds., *Handbooks of Applied Linguistics. Issue 2: Interpersonal Communication*. Mouton de Gruyter, pp. 509–540.

Locher, M. & Graham, S. (eds.). (2010). *Interpersonal Pragmatics*. Walter de Gruyter.

Locher, M. & Schnurr, S. (2017). (Im) politeness in health settings. In J. Culpeper, M. Haugh & D. Kádár, eds., *The Palgrave Handbook of Linguistic (Im) politeness*. Palgrave Macmillan, pp. 689–711.

Locher, M. & Watts, R. (2005). Politeness theory and relational work. *Journal of Politeness Research*, 1, 9–33.

Lorenzo-Dus, N., Garcés-Conejos Blitvich, P. & Bou-Franch, P. (2011). On-line polylogues and impoliteness: The case of postings sent in response to the Obama Reggaeton YouTube video. *Journal of pragmatics*, 43(10), 2578–2593.

Marlow, M. L. (2017). Public discourse and intergroup communication. *Oxford Research Encyclopedia of Communication*. https://oxfordre.com/commu nication/display/10.1093/acrefore/9780190228613.001.0001/acrefore-9780190228613-e-420.

McWhorter, J. (2021). Stay woke. The right can be iliberal too. www.nytimes .com/2022/01/25/opinion/woke-free-speech.html.

Márquez Reiter, R. & Bou-Franch, P. (2017). (Im) politeness in service encounters. In J. Culpeper, M. Haugh & D. Kádár, eds., *The Palgrave Handbook of Linguistic (Im)politeness*. Palgrave Macmillan, pp. 661–687.

Márquez-Reiter, R. M. & Placencia, M. E. (2005). *Spanish Pragmatics*. Palgrave Macmillan.

Marwick, A. & boyd, D. (2011). I tweet honestly, I tweet passionately: Twitter users, context collapse, and the imagined audience. *New Media & Society*, 13(1), 114–133.

Matsumoto, Y. (1988). Reexamination of the universality of face. *Journal of Pragmatics*, 12, 403–426.

Miller, C. R. (1984). Genre as social action. *Quarterly Journal of Speech*, 70(2), 151–167.

Miller, C. R. (2015). Genre as social action (1984) revisited 30 years later (2014). *Letras & Letras*, 31(3), 56–72.

Miller, E. R. (2013). Positioning selves, doing relational work and constructing identities in interview talk. *Journal of Politeness Research*, 9(1), 75–95.

Mills, S. (2003). *Class, Gender and Politeness*. Cambridge University Press.

Monroe, A. & Ashby Plant, E. (2019). The dark side of morality: Prioritizing sanctity over care motivates denial of mind and prejudice toward sexual outgroups. *Journal of Experimental Psychology: General*, 148(2), 342–360.

Morgan, M. (2010). The presentation of indirectness and power in everyday life. *Journal of Pragmatics*, 42(2), 283–291.

Mueller, T. S. (2021). Blame, then shame? Psychological predictors in cancel culture behavior. *The Social Science Journal*, 1–14. DOI: 10.1080/03623319.2021.1949552.

Ng, E. (2020). No grand pronouncements here … : Reflections on cancel culture and digital media participation. *Television & New Media*, 21(6), 621–627.

Norris, P. (2023). Cancel culture: Myth or reality? *Political Studies*, 71, 145–174.

Noyes, A. & Dunham, Y. (2017). Mutual intentions as a causal framework for social groups. *Cognition*, 162, 133–142.

Nwoye, O. (1992). Linguistics politeness and socio-cultural variations of the notion of face. *Journal of Pragmatics*, 18, 309–328.

O'Driscoll, J. (2017). Face and (im) politeness. In J. Culpeper, M. Haugh & D. Kádár, eds., *The Palgrave Handbook of Linguistic (Im)politeness*. Palgrave Macmillan, pp. 89–118.

Orlikowski, W. J. & Yates, J. (1994). Genre repertoire: The structuring of communicative practices in organizations. *Administrative Science Quarterly*, 39, 541–574.

Pappacharissi, Z. (2011). *A Networked Self*. Routledge.

Pennycook, A. (2010). *Language as a Local Practice*. Routledge.

Percy-Smith, B. & Matthews, H. (2001). Tyrannical spaces: Young people, bullying and urban neighbourhoods. *Local Environment*, 6(1), 49–63.

Peters, M. A. & Besley, T. A. (2014). Social exclusion/inclusion: Foucault's analytics of exclusion, the political ecology of social inclusion and the legitimation of inclusive education. *Open Review of Educational Research*, 1(1), 99–115.

Pires, R. P. (2012). 0 problema da ordem [The problem of order]. *Sociologia, Problemas e Praticas*, 69, 31–45.

Polletta, F. & Jasper, J. (2001). Collective identity and social movements. *Annual Review of Sociology*, 27(1), 283–305.

Rao, H. & Dutta, S. (2012). Free spaces as organizational weapons of the weak: Religious festivals and regimental mutinies in the 1857 Bengal Native Army. *Administrative Science Quarterly*, 57(4), 625–668.

Rawls, A. W. (2005). Garfinkel's conception of time. *Time & Society*, 14(2-3), 163–190.

Reichl, F. (2019). From vigilantism to digilantism? In B. Akhgar, P. Bayerl & G. Leventakis, eds., *Social Media Strategy in Policing*. Springer, pp. 117–138.

Rempala, K., Hornewer, M. & Samoska, S. (2020). The dark side of morality: Grayer than you think? *AJOB Neuroscience*, 11(4), 295–297.

Reicher, S. D., Spears, R. & Postmes, T. (1995). A social identity model of deindividuation phenomena. *European Review of Social Psychology*, 6(1), 161–198.

Romano, A. (2019). Why we can't stop fighting about cancel culture:Is cancel culture a mob mentality, or a long overdue way of speaking truth to power? *Vox*. www.vox.com/culture/2019/12/30/20879720/what-is-cancel-culture-explained-history-debate.

Romano, A. (2021). The second wave of cancel culture. *Vox*. www.vox.com/22384308/cancel-culture-free-speech-accountability-debate.

Salmani-Nodoushan, M. A. (2007). Politeness markers in Persian requestives. *The Linguistics Journal*, 2, 43–68.

Saint-Louis, H. (2021). Understanding cancel culture: Normative and unequal sanctioning. *Firstmonday*, 26(7). https://firstmonday.org/ojs/index.php/fm/article/view/10891/11211.

Schweikard, D. P. & Schmid, H. B. (2021). Collective intentionality. In E. N. Zalta, ed., *The Stanford Encyclopedia of Philosophy* (Fall 2021 ed.). https://plato.stanford.edu/archives/fall2021/entries/collective-intentionality/.

Scollon, R., & Scollon, S. W. (2003). *Discourses in Place: Language in the Material World*. Routledge.

Searle, J. (2010). *Making the Social World: The Structure of Human Civilization*. Oxford University Press.

Serpa, S. & Ferreira, C. M. (2019). Micro, meso and macro-levels of social analysis. *International Journal of Social Science Studies*, 7(3), 120–124.

Shaw, F. (2012). The politics of blogs: Theories of discursive activism online. *Media International Australia*, 142(1), 41–49.

Sifianou, M. (1999). *Politeness Phenomena in England and Greece: A Cross-cultural Perspective*. Oxford University Press.

Sifianou, M. (2011). On the concept of face and politeness. In F. Bargiela-Chiappini & D. Kádár, eds., *Politeness across Cultures*. Palgrave Macmillan, pp. 42–58.

Sorell, T. (2019). Scambaiting on the spectrum of digilantism. *Criminal Justice Ethics*, 38(3), 153–175.

Spencer-Oatey, H. (2005). (Im)Politeness, face and perceptions of rapport: Unpackaging their bases and interrelationships. *Journal of Politeness Research*, 1(1), 95−119.

Spencer-Oatey, H. (2007). Theories of identity and the analysis of face. *Journal of Pragmatics*, 39, 639−656.

Spinuzzi, C. (2004). Describing assemblages: Genre sets, systems, repertoires, and ecologies. Computer Writing and Research Lab. www.dwrl.utexas .edu/old/content/describing-assemblages.html.

Spinuzzi, C. & Zachry, M. (2000). Genre ecologies: An open-system approach to understanding and constructing documentation. *ACM Journal of Computer Documentation*, 24(3), 169–181.

Stets, J. & Burke, P. (2000). Identity theory and social identity theory. *Social Psychology Quarterly*, 63,224–237.

Straka, B., Stanaland, A., Tomasello, T. & Gaither, S. (2021). Who can be in a group? 3-to 5-year-old children construe realistic social groups through mutual intentionality. *Cognitive Development*, 60, 101097. https://doi.org/ 10.1016/j.cogdev.2021.101097

Swales, J. M. (1990). *Genre Analysis: English in Academic and Research Settings*. Cambridge University Press.

Swales, J. M. (2004). *Research Genres: Explorations and Applications*. Cambridge University Press.

Tajfel, H. (1979). Individuals and groups in social psychology. *British Journal of Social and Clinical Psychology*, 18(2), 183–190.

Tajfel, H., Turner, J. (1979/2004). An integrative theory of intergroup conflict. In M.J. Hatch & M. Schultz, eds., *Organizational Identity: A Reader*. Oxford University Press, pp. 56–65.

Tardy, C. (2009). *Building Genre Knowledge*. Parlor Press LLC.

Thi Nguyen, C. & Strohl, M. (2019). Cultural appropriation and the intimacy of groups. *Philosophical Studies*, 176(4), 981–1002.

Thiele, M. (2021). Political correctness and cancel culture–a question of power. *Journalism Research*, 4(1), 50–57.

Thorne, S. L. & Reinhardt, J. (2008). "Bridging activities," new media literacies, and advanced foreign language proficiency. *Calico Journal*, 25(3), 558–572.

Thornton, P. (2018). A critique of linguistic capitalism: Provocation/intervention. *Geohumanities*, 4(2), 417–437.

Tollefsen, D. (2002). Collective intentionality and the social sciences. *Philosophy of the Social Sciences*, 32(1), 25–50.

Tollefsen, D. P. (2015). *Groups as Agents*. John Wiley & Sons.

Tomasello, M. (2018). How we learned to put our fate in one another's hands: The origins of morality. *Scientific American*, 319(3), 70–75.

Tomasello, M., Melis, A. P., Tennie, C., Wyman, E. & Herrmann, E. (2012). Two key steps in the evolution of human cooperation: The interdependence hypothesis. *Current Anthropology*, 53(6), 673–692.

Tomasello, M. & Rakoczy, H. (2003). What makes human cognition unique? From individual to shared to collective intentionality. *Mind & Language*, 18(2), 121–147.

Tuomela, R. (2004). Group knowledge analyzed. *Episteme*, *1*(2), 109–127.

Tuomela, R. (2007). *The Philosophy of Sociality: The Shared Point of View*. Oxford University Press.

Tuomela, R. (2011). An account of group knowledge. *Collective Epistemology*, 75-117.

Tuomela, R. (2013). *Social Ontology: Collective Intentionality and Group Agents*. Oxford University Press.

Tuomela, R. (2017). Non-reductive views of shared intention. In M. Jankovic & K. Ludwig, eds., *The Routledge Handbook of Collective Intentionality*. Routledge, pp. 25–33.

Turner, J. & Stets, J. (2006). Moral emotions. In J. Stets & J. Turner, eds., *Handbook of the Sociology of Emotions: Volume II*. Springer, pp. 544–566.

Vähämaa, M. (2013). Groups as epistemic communities: Social forces and affect as antecedents to knowledge. *Social Epistemology*, 27(1), 3–20.

van Dijk, T. A. (1995). Power and the news media. *Political Communication and Action*, 6(1), 9–36.

Varis, P. & van Nuenen, T. (2017). The internet, language, and virtual interactions. In O. García, N. Flores & M. Spotti, eds.,*The Oxford Handbook of Language and Society*. Oxford University Press, pp. 473–488.

Vásquez, C. (2011). Complaints online: The case of TripAdvisor. *Journal of Pragmatics*, 43(6), 1707–1717.

Velasco, J. C. (2020). You are cancelled: Virtual collective consciousness and the emergence of cancel culture as ideological purging. *Rupkatha Journal on Interdisciplinary Studies in Humanities*, 12(5), 48–68.

Vogels, E. (2022). A growing share of Americans are familiar with "Cancel Culture." Pew Research Center. www.pewresearch.org/fact-tank/2022/06/09/a-growing-share-of-americans-are-familiar-with-cancel-culture/.

Vogels, E., Anderson, M., Porteus, M. et al. (2021). Americans and "Cancel Culture": Where some see calls for accountability, others see censorship, punishment. www.pewresearch.org/internet/2021/05/19/americans-and-cancel-culture-where-some-see-calls-for-accountability-others-see-cen sorship-punishment/.

Wang, J. & Spencer-Oatey, H. (2015). The gains and losses of face in ongoing intercultural interaction: A case study of Chinese participant perspectives. *Journal of Pragmatics*, 89, 50–65.

Watts, R. J. (2003). *Politeness*. Cambridge University Press.

Watson-Jones, R. E. & Legare, C. H. (2016). The social functions of group rituals. *Current Directions in Psychological Science*, 25(1), 42–46.

Weir, R. (2014). Social ontology: Collective intentionality and group agents by Raimo Tuomela. *Studies in Social and Political Thought*, 23, 78–81.

Wesselmann, E. D., Wirth, J. H., Pryor, J. B., Reeder, G. D. & Williams, K. D. (2013). When do we ostracize? *Social Psychological and Personality Science*, 4(1), 108–115.

Workman, C. I., Yoder, K. J. & Decety, J. (2020). The dark side of morality– Neural mechanisms underpinning moral convictions and support for vio- lence. *AJOB Neuroscience*, 11(4), 269–284.

Zappavigna, M. (2014). Enacting identity in microblogging through ambient affiliation. *Discourse & Communication*, 8(2), 209–228.

Wray, K. B. (2001). Collective belief and acceptance. *Synthese*, 129(3), 319–333.

Zeng, J. & Abidin, C. (2021). "# OkBoomer, time to meet the Zoomers": Studying the memefication of intergenerational politics on TikTok. *Information, Communication & Society*, 24(16), 2459–2481.

Acknowledgments

I would like to express my sincere gratitude to the Elements in Pragmatics series editors, Professor Jonathan Culpeper and Professor Michael Haugh, for their encouragement and support. I am also deeply grateful to Professors Nuria Lorenzo-Dus (University of Swansea) and Maria Sifianou (National and Kapodistrian University of Athens) who provided very insightful feedback on an earlier version of this Element and are always there, ready to help. I would also like to recognize Mouli Chattaraj, M.A., my research assistant, for her diligence. Special thanks go to Thomas L. Blitvich, my sounding board for academic and life in general projects.

Cambridge Elements ☰

Pragmatics

Jonathan Culpeper
Lancaster University, UK
Jonathan Culpeper is Professor of English Language and Linguistics in the Department of Linguistics and English Language at Lancaster University, UK. A former co-editor-in-chief of the *Journal of Pragmatics* (2009–14), with research spanning multiple areas within pragmatics, his major publications include: *Impoliteness: Using Language to Cause Offence* (2011, CUP) and *Pragmatics and the English Language* (2014, Palgrave; with Michael Haugh).

Michael Haugh
University of Queensland, Australia
Michael Haugh is Professor of Linguistics and Applied Linguistics in the School of Languages and Cultures at the University of Queensland, Australia. A former co-editor-in-chief of the *Journal of Pragmatics* (2015–2020), with research spanning multiple areas within pragmatics, his major publications include: *Understanding Politeness* (2013, CUP; with Dániel Kádár), *Pragmatics and the English Language* (2014, Palgrave; with Jonathan Culpeper), and *Im/politeness Implicatures* (2015, Mouton de Gruyter).

Advisory Board

About the Series
The Cambridge Elements in Pragmatics series showcases dynamic and high-quality original, concise and accessible scholarly works. Written for a broad pragmatics readership it encourages dialogue across different perspectives on language use. It is a forum for cutting-edge work in pragmatics: consolidating theory (especially through cross-fertilization), leading the development of new methods, and advancing innovative topics in pragmatics.

Cambridge Elements ≡

Pragmatics

Printed in the United States
by Baker & Taylor Publisher Services